If you think you know how advertising works, think again. This book is fascinating, provocative and inspiring. It's a joy to read.

Jim Carroll, Chairman, BBH London

The Anatomy of Humbug is an easy and enjoyable read, and the message is new, valid and useful. No-one has previously discussed the various "practitioner theories" of advertising so comprehensively. It's a great story, and I learned a lot.

Patrick Barwise, Emeritus Professor of Management and Marketing, London Business School.

I love this book as it does precisely what it says on the cover; not only is 'humbug' de-constructed, but clarity shines through. Too few executives can really articulate the case for consistent advertising to their peers or shareholders, but reading this book will improve this deficit immeasurably.

Martin Glenn, CEO, United Biscuits

Paul Feldwick examines how we all think advertising works and the history of why we think that way. He, subtly, gently and wisely will make you realise that, actually, you don't really know and have just been getting on with it. There's a lot of useful learning in this little book.

Russell Davies, Director of Strategy, Government Digital Service

A thoughtful and beautifully written reflection on the history of advertising practice. Feldwick explores how the narratives that agencies have used to sell their work still influence current beliefs about how advertising works, and offers his own perspective. Advertising practitioners that read this book may find themselves questioning tenets they have long taken for granted.

Nigel Hollis, Chief Global Analyst, Millward Brown

An elegant overview of the history of advertising theory, with the added joy of being filtered through the immense wisdom, experience and brain of this advertising guru. It shows that successful advertising is the product of rich, complex, even paradoxical approaches - which maybe explains why advertising attracts people who would be comfortable round a dinner table with both Freud and P.T.Barnum. In a world seemingly addicted to binary solutions, this book will help you avoid becoming an advertising fashion victim, to learn from the past in order to develop your own successful approach to advertising.

Tess Alps, Chair, Thinkbox

This is a genuinely original book, unlike anything ever written about advertising. Publicist P.T.Barnum, research guru Ernest Dichter, PR giant Edward Bernays, as well as advertising heroes, Bill Bernbach and David Ogilvy, are just a few of the huge cast of characters that leap off the page ... readers will be amazed at the intellectual energy, passion and eccentricity the business has excited since its earliest days. Feldwick writes with clarity and wit: his book should required reading for anyone in the business of communication.

Judie Lannon, Editor, Market Leader.

This is a unique and extraordinary book for a very simple reason: it is a dispassionate account of the advertising industry, written by an insider, which charts the often wide gulf between how we think advertising ought to work and how it really does.

Rory Sutherland, Vice Chairman, Ogilvy London.

The
Anatomy
of
Humbug

How to Think Differently About Advertising

Paul Feldwick

Matador
9 Priory Business Park
Kibworth Beauchamp
Leicestershire LE8 0RX, UK
Tel: (+44) 116 279 2299
Fax: (+44) 116 279 2277
Email: books@troubador.co.uk
Web: www.troubador.co.uk/matador

ISBN 978-1784621-926

British Library Cataloguing in Publication Data.
A catalogue record for this book is available from the British Library.

Typeset in Chaparral Pro by Troubador Publishing Ltd

Matador is an imprint of Troubador Publishing Ltd

Ideas we have, and do not know we have, have us.

James Hillman, *Kinds of Power*, p.18

Contents

Foreword

I n Chapter Ten of this wonderfully sane book, Paul Feldwick remembers giving a lecture at an advertising seminar in Istanbul. He was presenting several case histories from the IPA Advertising Effectiveness Awards archive: the world's most rigorously documented instances of advertising having demonstrably and unarguably delivered commercial success as measured by sales, share of market, profit and return on investment. After one such case, a leading figure in Turkish research circles raised her hand and said with absolute conviction, 'It is not possible that this campaign was successful. The commercial contains no consumer benefit.' (No doubt she would also have insisted that bumblebees can't fly.)

Other than advertising, there can't be many activities where theory and practice diverge so widely and so frequently. Like Paul, I came into advertising knowing nothing. And though the agency I joined, J. Walter Thompson, was far more academically inclined than most (it had been dubbed 'the University of Advertising' in the US before World War II) it offered me no immediate training. I was expected to write an advertisement before lunch on my first day – and I did. The only guidance I was given, and that much later, was an introduction to what was called The

Thompson T-Square. This was a set of simple questions designed to concentrate the copywriter's mind on the essentials and was, as the name implied, intended as a practical tool. The questions were: What are we selling? To whom are we selling it? Where are we selling it? When are we selling it? How are we selling it?

It was, and remains, a useful checklist for anyone setting out to write an advertisement for anything in any medium – and it's not as simplistic as it seems at first sight. In answering *What are we selling?*, for example, we were encouraged to consider not just the physical product but also what that product might represent to its users. A considered answer for Parker pens, for instance, would be expected to go far beyond 'a prestigious writing instrument' and explore the pen's potential as a gift and the pleasure it could deliver to the recipient. But the T-Square was also explicitly intended to lead to the identification of The Proposition, 'the core of every advertisement': 'The Proposition is the strongest competitive promise on behalf of a product or service that can be made to the consumer in terms of his (sic) own self-interest. It must be truthful, demonstrable and unique – clearly elevating the product or service over the competition.' Since the T-Square dated back to the reign of Stanley Resor (who had bought the company from James Walter Thompson himself in 1916, and stayed with it until he died in 1961), this emphasis on a unique competitive consumer proposition probably pre-dated Rosser Reeves's adoption of the USP on behalf of the Ted Bates agency in the late 1950s. Yet I don't remember anyone at JWT, then or later, insisting that every campaign for every client contained an explicit competitive promise. Round the world, the agency found the T-Square questions helpful because they encouraged not only a certain discipline of thought but also the exercise of open-ended speculation and imagination. But when it came to instructions about what to put into every advertisement – what every advertisement should contain – the Resor directive was broadly ignored. It wasn't ignored militantly or even consciously – it just, collectively, must have seemed restrictive and wrong.

Then as now, there were many examples of advertising campaigns that were clearly extremely successful in commercial terms but which contained no overt and demonstrable consumer promise. (The first Katie and Philip TV campaign for Oxo in the UK was a huge success over a great many years, yet perhaps only one Turkish researcher would have credited that success entirely to the line, 'Oxo Gives a Meal Man-Appeal!'.)

As Paul entertainingly recounts, in the hundred-year-plus history of advertising, just about every doctrine to do with advertising content has been shown to be wanting: many may hold true in some instances, perhaps, but none in all. Some of them were designed (like Bates's Unique Selling Proposition) mainly to promote the agency that espoused them; and some are the children of academics who would dearly like the business of advertising to be an exact science. I am reminded of what the great E.F. Schumacher had to say in *Small is Beautiful* (1973): 'Economics, and even more so applied economics, is not an exact science; it is, in fact, or ought to be, something much greater: a branch of wisdom.' If it didn't sound so pretentious - which Paul Feldwick never is - much the same might be said about advertising.

But I think Paul sells himself short when he says, 'This is not a book about how advertising works. This is a book about how people think advertising works'. And so it is; but by cataloguing the many different thoughts and theories that advertising has attracted over the last hundred years, and by continually returning to advertising as it is rather than advertising as the theorists would like it to be, he reveals the reality far more usefully than if he had set out specifically to do so.

One last hint: please reserve your judgement on the title until you've read Paul's reasons for having chosen it.

Jeremy Bullmore

Prologue:

How the Ad Industry Thinks about its Past

So-called practical men, who have never knowingly been exposed to an intellectual influence in their lives, are invariably the slaves of some defunct economist.

John Maynard Keynes, *The General Theory of Employment, Interest and Money.*

.

Prologue:

How the Ad Industry Thinks about its Past

In 1974 I joined Boase Massimi Pollitt (BMP), a rising and extremely successful London agency with about sixty staff. If you want to picture the offices I showed up at, that October morning, as a TV drama, it was much more *Life on Mars* than *Mad Men*: the men swaggering and loud in big hair, big ties and big lapels, the women mostly ensconced behind IBM Golfball typewriters whose deafening clatter filled the air along with plenty of cigarette smoke and bad language. Photocopiers and pocket calculators were still recent inventions. We didn't, of course, have mobile phones, personal computers, email, the web. TV commercials, which had only been in colour for a couple of years, were shot on 35 mm stock which had to be viewed on the massive double head projector in the room called The Cinema. Artwork was pasted up in the studio with a lot of cow gum. Presentations required several hundredweight of 20x30 polyboard which had to be sent out to a studio forty-eight hours ahead of the meeting. And so on....

It occurs to me now that if, on that first day, I'd met someone who proudly told me they had started in advertising forty years before me – that is, in 1934 – they would have appeared to me as a personage of extraordinary antiquity. And if they'd started reminiscing about how advertising used to be before the advent of television, in the days when illustrations had to be cut as printer's blocks, physically copied and sent to each publication, when copywriters and art directors sat on separate floors and communicated through ill-tempered memos, I would probably have found it all quite irrelevant to me. In fact, I don't remember meeting anyone, then or since, who worked in advertising before the Second World War – to me, when I started, even the sixties felt like a bygone age of narrow lapels and beehive hairdo's. Because advertising then, just as much as today if not more so, was a young person's business. Our managing director was 28; the only people in the agency over 30 were two of the founder directors, both around 40, and a rather avuncular Chairman who didn't do much: he might have been fifty. Today, half the staff in IPA agencies are under 30, and only 5% over 50.

Like my colleagues and my bosses, I had no formal training in advertising. Such training as then existed we heartily despised as irrelevant. We prided ourselves on our unique talents and superior brains, and we had immense confidence, bordering on arrogance. For the most part this combination seems to have served us rather well. We were one of the best agencies in town (we would have said without a doubt, *the* best), and even with hindsight I'd claim we produced many of the most famous and effective campaigns of the seventies and eighties. What did we need to learn from books? Or from our predecessors in the ad business?

On the basis of thirty years' experience across the ad industry all over the world, I would say that our attitude to the past was not untypical: the default position for most advertising people was, and still is, that the past is irrelevant. I've already touched on some possible reasons for this. It's a young person's business, and even if you survive to the age of fifty in it, you still think you are 27 because you are surrounded by 27 year olds (I did, anyway). Its authority as a profession is rather shaky, without the basis in 'technical rationality' or case law that legal or medical professions claim – so to compensate, a successful performance of confidence and self-belief has always gone a long way. But these don't fully explain the particular ways in which advertising chooses to ignore its own past.

You could say that advertising people ignore their own history simply because they never think about it, but I don't think that properly explains the relationship they have constructed towards the past. It might be more accurate to say that advertising people have created implicit narratives that give them permission not to think about the past - and if by chance they do ever think about the past, they do so safely through the lens of one of these narratives. What I mean by this will, I hope, become clearer as I describe what these narratives are; I'm thinking of three main kinds of story that the ad industry tells itself about its own past, which I shall call:

- The Enlightenment narrative
- The Golden Age narrative
- The Year Zero narrative

Let me explain what I mean by each of these.

The Enlightenment Narrative

The Enlightenment narrative can be summed up as follows: *The past was primitive, but now we are enlightened.* I think this describes my own early experiences at BMP. We genuinely thought we had found new ways of doing things, we fiercely believed in their rightness, and even more fiercely in the wrongness of everything we were reacting against. We rejected the past like a heresy (and yes, that was the sort of word we used).

But that was just our own local and specific version of the Enlightenment narrative, which has a long history in advertising. Here is a famous example:

> The time has come when advertising has in some hands reached the status of a science. It is based on fixed principles and is reasonably exact. The causes and effects have been analyzed until they are well understood. The correct methods of procedure have been proved and established. We know what is most effective, and we act on basic laws.
>
> Advertising, once a gamble, has thus become, under able direction, one of the safest of business ventures.

This is the opening passage of Claude Hopkins's 1923 book, *Scientific Advertising.* Tellingly, I have used this in many teaching sessions with advertising professionals over the years and hardly anyone has ever recognised it – worse, hardly anyone has ever heard of Claude Hopkins. Yet this is the best selling advertising book of all time, selling over eight million copies, and David Ogilvy said no-one should work in advertising until they had read it seven times. (Ogilvy is rare among admen for the honour he paid to his predecessors.)

Hopkins's principles, based on mail order response, may be the antithesis of what we worked to at BMP in the seventies - but like us, he expresses an absolute confidence that he now knows the right way to go about advertising. Everything before this is dismissed as primitive and haphazard – 'advertising, once a gamble'. And if you knew no better, you might suppose Hopkins had a point: surely anything before 1923 must have been the dark ages of advertising? Yet for decades before Hopkins wrote, huge sums were spent on advertising which was creative, sophisticated, and undeniably effective, a fact to which men like William Hesketh Lever and John Wanamaker owed their immense fortunes.

The Enlightenment narrative always overclaims for the power of new approaches, whatever they are, and it equally dismisses anything prior as obsolete. Twenty years before Hopkins wrote, another enlightenment myth was popularised in the story of how John E. Kennedy blagged his way into the office of Albert Lasker, the MD of the Lord and Thomas agency, to tell him that advertising was 'salesmanship in print', a formula that was supposed to make all others history. Later Enlightenment narratives could include the rise, and later the fall, of Motivation Research in the 1950s; Rosser Reeves's theory of the Unique Selling Proposition in the 1960s; and at about the same time, the so-called 'creative revolution' (more of all these stories later). And more recently, the popularity of market modelling and data analytics, neuroscience, and behavioural economics.

Within this kind of narrative framework, today's 'enlightenment' is often doomed to become tomorrow's obsolete mumbo-jumbo. And that is the central danger of this way of thinking. Over time we should expect to make new discoveries and get better at what we do. But we don't get better by expecting too much from the latest craze, while ignoring everything that's been achieved in the past.

The Enlightenment narrative has always been popular because it makes things appear much simpler than they are. It takes one narrow perspective and says 'this is all you need', generally attaching a high premium to novelty. It rewrites history so that everything else is positioned as irrelevant and wrong, ignoring any inconvenient facts. And the payoff is that, in order to be an expert in advertising, you don't need to pretend to understand anything other than the latest fashion; you only need to assert with sufficient confidence that everything else is old hat.

The Enlightenment narrative is still with us, but I think it is harder to sustain on its own than it used to be. Ad people today are less likely to have the same sense that we did in 1974 that things had never been better. So to a large extent the Enlightenment narrative as I have described it has today been superseded by the Year Zero narrative, which I shall describe in a moment. And part of the reason for this change has been the corresponding rise of my second narrative -

The Golden Age Narrative

In a recent survey of 500 UK advertising executives, cited in *Campaign*, more than 70% believed that the best years of the advertising industry were in the past. I don't have more detail of that survey, but I can fill it out a bit from my own contacts with agencies and my reading of the trade press. There's a definite tendency to admire – sometimes even to fetishise – ads from the past, though this is often very selective, with the same ads repeatedly selected as points of reference: the DDB New York campaigns from the sixties, the Levi's ads from the eighties, the Guinness Surfer, the Smash Martians. Now I'm all in favour of appreciating ads from the past, and we should do it more. But what strikes me about this narrative is the way it looks back on the canonical campaigns with a certain nostalgia, and perhaps even a certain despair. It does feel like the original 'Golden Age' myth, the ancient Greeks who believed they were living at a time when things had already, inevitably, deteriorated, and could never be restored. While today's advertising professionals may dream of producing ads that in their view will emulate these models, they are more likely to talk about why that is so much more difficult today, perhaps even impossible. They complain about the dominance of pre-testing, the risk-averse mindset of their clients, the baleful influence of procurement departments, the lack of money and the lack of time, the agency's powerlessness to change things. Back in the seventies, or whenever, the narrative goes, it was easy to produce great work: agencies were treated with respect, creative people were treated like gods, everyone had long lunches and went home early, clients bought whatever they were offered and were grateful, or else they were told to fuck off. And today.....

These excuses have enough truth in them to sound plausible. Agencies – the best ones, anyway - were perhaps

9

more confident and assertive, more prepared to stand up for what they believed was best. The business was more prosperous, and there certainly was more time for lunch (which was where a lot of the real work got done). But the idea of the Golden Age is, to put it kindly, a gross exaggeration. The business of getting agency and client to agree was not obviously simpler than it is today, the gestation of the great campaigns was almost invariably long and painful and uncertain, and we did all work long hours and experience stress. (Back in 1958, Martin Mayer wrote that in agencies 'the hours are long to the point of brutishness', p.21.)

Maybe the business today is less fun and less rewarding than it was forty years ago; maybe the overall quality of the work has deteriorated. And if these things are true, I do not have any simple solutions as to how they might be improved. But I believe that the narrative of the Golden Age as I have described it is fundamentally unhelpful. It is a *disempowering* narrative. It functions so that today's advertising people can demonstrate to themselves that they have excellent taste and know exactly what they would like to be producing for their clients, while at the same time acknowledging that they don't – and putting the blame for that on somebody else.

You'll have noticed that the Enlightenment narrative and the Golden Age narrative are almost exact opposites – one says the past was primitive, the other that the past was wonderful. So how does the industry manage to live with two dominant narratives that fundamentally appear to contradict each other? There are at least a couple of ways this is accomplished.

One version, especially popular among creative departments, is a story which combines a version of the Enlightenment narrative – but located in the past – with the Golden Age narrative. This is the sub-narrative of the 'creative revolution', and it's most clearly articulated in Andrew Cracknell's recent book, *The Real Mad Men* (its subtitle - 'the remarkable true story of Madison Avenue's golden age, when a handful of renegades changed advertising for ever' – pretty much says it all.) The first part, the enlightenment part, goes like this. Prior to Bill Bernbach, all advertising was unremittingly crap - in the words of Fred Danzig's preface to Cracknell's book, 'brain-jarring repetition and hyperbole'. Then Bernbach came along and changed all this with 'good taste, humour, and amiable messages', followed by a string of other creative heroes like Papert Koenig Lois, Carl Ally and Jerry della Femina, and in London Collett Dickenson Pearce (and BMP). A similar narrative informs Sam Delaney's book about UK advertising in the sixties and seventies, *Get Smashed*.

Now these are both well researched and entertaining books, well worth reading for the rich detail they contain of important periods in advertising's history: and they've both been helpful to me. But I'm afraid I have to take issue with the partial view of history they present. In Stephen Fox's earlier and much more rounded history of US advertising, *The Mirror Men*, the chapter called 'The Creative Revolution' deals with three men, of whom Bernbach is only one; the others are David Ogilvy and Raymond Rubicam. Ogilvy himself wrote that 'the so-called Creative Revolution, usually ascribed to Bill Bernbach and myself in the fifties, could equally well have been ascribed to N.W.Ayer and Young & Rubicam in the thirties' (Ogilvy, p.7). One historian even identifies a shift in copy style from 'hard sell' to 'human interest' as early as 1920 (Marchand, pp.10-12). Fox suggests that such shifts in approach have been cyclic throughout advertising history, but it may be just as true to say that creativity, 'good taste, humour and amiable messages', have always been the preferred style of certain advertising practitioners – while others have been equally attached to the very different 'hard sell' techniques, and others to simple 'fame'. To put Bernbach into context, go back to Martin Mayer's brilliant contemporary study of the 1950s US advertising industry, *Madison Avenue USA*, to get a feel for what a diverse, innovative, intellectual and creative ferment that decade really was. However much you choose to admire their work, any narrative that positions DDB New York in the sixties as a unique, even redemptive event in the history of advertising is dangerously misleading.

Having located the enlightenment moment safely in the past – somewhere between fifty and sixty years ago now – the subsequent story of the passing of the golden age is told in the epilogue to *The Real Mad Men*, which laments the end of a 'bubbly, sun-dappled decade' (the Creative Revolution has now been located in the 1960s), and evokes the Vietnam War, the Manson murders, and the rise of Marion Harper's Interpublic agency group as the turning of the tide. It makes a neat ending – but it's not the only narrative that we have to believe.

There is another, and even more pervasive story which elegantly enables today's ad exec to escape the complications of the past, without having to decide whether it was Golden Age or Dark Ages. This narrative is simple – whatever happened in the past, the world has now changed so much that it's all completely irrelevant. This is the dominant narrative today and I call it

The Year Zero Narrative

The idea that 'the world has changed and the old rules no longer apply' has been a popular one for a long time in marketing and advertising circles. It does indeed look a bit like the enlightenment narrative, but the difference is that here the change has been primarily dictated by external forces, rather than the author's new discovery – although most authors of this sort of thing do, usually, have a new discovery or radical new worldview, which just happens to fit the brave new world we're about to enter.

The external forces that are behind such stories are many and varied, but mostly focus around two themes. One is the changing nature of the consumer, about whom many things are asserted (but few usually demonstrated). The other, which in the past twenty years has become more and more dominant, is technological change and its impact on commerce and on communications. The two are often combined, as for instance in the claim that, because of the internet, today's consumer is more 'empowered' or more 'cynical'.

What you will notice about most of the writing on this subject is a great deal of broad assertion that some fundamental change is happening *right now*. The assertion is generally vague enough that it's hard to directly deny it. It may be nonsense, or it may be partially true – in which case it may have been equally true ten years ago, or a hundred years ago. But string together enough topical anecdotes, learned sounding riffs from cultural theorists and hip rhetoric, and few people will bother to argue with you. Here are two quotes to give the flavour:

> Crash! Boom! Bang!
> Welcome to the age of accidents. Welcome to the age of constant alarm bells where surprise is all and no one can predict what will happen tomorrow.

> A great phase in human society appears to be drawing to a close – the Age of Image.
> Some called it the society of the spectacle: a time saturated by images from the new media of cinema, magazines and television. These fused with the growth of leisure, lifestyle and mass-produced goods to create a Consumer Society. It's now being challenged by everyone from anti-globalization protestors to non-conformist Geeks.
> As one phase closes, another opens – the Age of Intellect.

I've no doubt people are writing plenty more of this stuff today. As it happens, these are from the opening sections of books published in 2000 and 2002 respectively. The first, *Funky Business*, by Jonas Ridderstråle and Kjelle Nordström, concludes that in this new 'age of accidents' 'the only way to create real profit is to attract the emotional rather than rational consumer ... by appealing to their feelings and fantasy'. The second, John Grant's *After Image*, argues that the 'Age of Image' is dead: 'The truth about brand image is that it was a pack of lies... How did people get taken in for fifty years by these fantasies?'. One presents, as new, a proposition that I incline to agree with, but don't see anything remotely new in; the other announces, also as new, the exact opposite, and the fact that I don't believe it for a moment is not really important. As usual in this kind of writing, both banal platitudes and eccentric speculation are presented as evidence for 'the way the world has changed'.

Indulge my rant for a moment, because these portentous generalisations about the consumer do make me a bit angry – not just because they're so obviously spurious, but because of the arrogance and contempt for the public which they often imply. 'How did people get taken in for fifty years by these fantasies?' – Well, obviously because they were stupid. And now suddenly, mysteriously, they're not. Except, even more mysteriously, they're still buying brands: they're still visiting Starbucks and McDonald's, drinking Coca-Cola, and thinking how cool Apple is. In 2010, Professor Richard Scase of the University of Kent wrote an article in the respected journal *Market Leader* about what he called 'the iPod generation':

> ...the iPod generation lives in an almost completely digitalised world... in which interpersonal communication is spontaneous, egalitarian, and supportive of intense information and decision making flows... The iPod generation is in control. No-one tells them what to buy... As consumers they are not persuaded by the marketing and selling strategies of corporations.

The author seems quite unconscious of the irony that he has chosen to name this fictitious generation 'who are not persuaded by the marketing and selling strategies of corporations' after a temporarily fashionable, premium priced and highly advertised – brand.

OK, rant over. You'll have gathered that I don't think much of claims that the consumer has fundamentally changed; and if you want to persuade me otherwise, I'd like much harder evidence than I've seen so far.

On the other hand, I couldn't really pretend that technology hasn't changed or that it hasn't had a major impact on commerce and communication during the last twenty years. The question is – do these changes, however wide reaching and important they are, support a narrative that renders the previous history of advertising irrelevant?

I want to argue, not just that they don't, but that the opposite is true – that we will only be able to respond adequately to the continuing rapid pace of change in commerce and communications if we understand the basic principles of how people are influenced by publicity. And we can best understand those principles if we're prepared to study both the theory and the practice that have been built up over the last hundred and fifty years. I am not so naive as to claim that online commerce is just a modern version of mail order, or that an email is no more than today's equivalent of a telegram, or that a banner ad is really just the same as an earpiece in a 1952 copy of the Evening Standard. But then again, I am not so stupid as to imagine they are totally different either. The Year Zero narrative is supported by focusing only on those things that have changed, and there are plenty of them – some of them may be big and important things and I'm not getting into an argument about which they are. But we can choose to focus also on those things that haven't changed – and there are plenty of those too. Let me suggest some broad headings:

- The emotional basis of decision making.
- People's interest in reading text.
- What makes people laugh or cry.
- The desire to share opinions with others.
- The need to contact someone in charge when things go wrong.
- Consumers' attention spans (despite wild claims to the contrary).
- Attitudes to being interrupted at the wrong moment.
- Buying decisions mediated by brands.
- Sometimes price is important, sometimes it isn't.
- The importance of Low Attention Processing in persuasion.
- Interest in relevant facts when making certain purchases.
- People over fifty have trouble reading small print.
- Susceptibility to sexual attractiveness.
- Enjoyment of music.
- Wanting to feel connected.
- Appreciation of good service and wanting to feel valued as a customer.

I suppose that none of these things has changed that much in over a hundred years (and you can I'm sure add to the list yourself). What's more, during that hundred year period, they have all been understood in some way and exploited by successful marketers – and screwed up by others. Although many things change over time, the fundamentals of how people learn, perceive, choose, and are able to influence each other, don't change – not even when they discover television, or mobile phones, or Twitter.

And the fundamental questions of advertising, in whatever medium, have similarly remained the same throughout its history. Are people more influenced by words or by pictures? Do you need to remember what you've seen or heard in order to be influenced by it? Do we choose based on our reason or our emotions, whatever we mean by those simple sounding terms? Is it important for advertising to be liked, and does it matter if people hate it? Does a successful ad need a single message, multiple messages, or no message at all? How much repetition does an ad need to be effective, and how much is too much? Is advertising an art, or a science, or something else?

If your narrative of advertising history is a Year Zero narrative, your answers to such questions will probably be based on 'common sense'. But that is only to say that they will be based on half-digested folk memories of some particular answer that someone you never heard of once gave in the past. What Keynes wrote in 1936 about economics is just as true of advertising:

> So-called practical men, who have never knowingly been exposed to an intellectual influence in their lives, are invariably the slaves of some defunct economist.

All of the words that we still use as common currency in planning advertising, concepts which even skilled professionals regard as self evident truths, have a historical beginning in a specific place and time, and come loaded with the baggage of a particular world view that we might or might not really want – I mean words like *impact, recall, proposition, attention, reason why, message, idea....* As long as we accept all this uncritically as just 'common sense', we are as Keynes said, slaves to it.

Among other drawbacks, we become slaves to mutually contradictory principles, which is one reason why advertising development is fraught with so many passionate arguments. When the client insists on factual copy and the creative director insists on an attention grabbing picture, neither will recognise that this is a standoff between a copywriter of the 1920s who honed his craft as a travelling preacher and snake oil salesman, and a college professor from the Mid-West who in the 1950s invented a highly lucrative but somewhat facile technique for evaluating press ads.

When I came into this business, like my colleagues I knew little of its past and cared less. But as I slowly, somewhat haphazardly began to uncover more about the history of advertising, I found that it was not just a fascinating story; I discovered that at every point it helped me make sense of the situations I found myself in daily in the course of my work. I realised that the dilemmas we were struggling with were not new – neither were most of the answers we produced. Our processes, our language, our research techniques – all the things we took most for granted – turned out to be hand-me-downs from the past. Our most fundamental assumptions, the ones we never questioned or never even articulated – they were the echoes of some long-dead copywriter with a gift for words. When we thought we were thinking for ourselves, we were most likely to be thinking only the thoughts of others – those same others who in our youthful arrogance we thought we were choosing to ignore. Year Zero thinking didn't just cast us adrift without direction; it trapped us, without our realising it, in directions not of our own choosing. Our ability to decide clearly where we want to go to in the future, I now believe, depends first of all on our understanding of where we and our predecessors have already been.

Maybe we did have it easier in the seventies. We were flying high, on a newly cresting wave of colour TV commercials with high production values which the public often agreed were 'better than the programmes' – we could get away with not thinking too much about history. But if today's changing media landscape is more challenging, complex, and unknown – which it certainly is – if the business is less fun, more highly stretched and stressed out – which it probably is – if these things are true, we can no longer hope to get away with flying by the seat of our pants. We need to be open to the lessons of history in order to deal adequately with the future. Rather than ignore history, or make up simple stories about it, I believe the advertising industry could be both more respectful of its past and more critical of it.

About this Book

This is not a book about 'how advertising works'. There was a time when I wanted to write that book; now I'm not so sure that it's a book that can really be written. This is a book about 'how people *think* – or *assume* - advertising works': about the different theories, or models, or maybe even metaphors that we, as practitioners, adopt when we try to think about advertising - as we can't avoid doing.

Although there is a lot of history in it, it's not intended as a history book. My purpose is entirely practical. I've written this book in the belief that it's only by understanding the historical roots of the assumptions we make about advertising that we can begin to free ourselves from being Keynesian 'slaves' to those assumptions. It's only when we realise that none of these theories, models or metaphors represents absolute truth, but is one of many 'ways of seeing' (which happens to be close to the original meaning of the Greek word *theoria*), that we can make use of any of them as a source of inspiration rather than be confined by it.

If all this sounds appalling to anyone who demands certainty in anything they do, I'm afraid that is exactly the way in which I am challenging them in this book to 'think differently about advertising'. There has been a rumbling debate for well over a hundred years now as to whether advertising should be considered an art or a science. But during that hundred years the notion of what science itself is has been radically transformed. From about the time of Descartes until the mid twentieth century, there was a fundamental assumption that science was a quest for certainty (Toulmin). This idea was easily translated to appeal to management's desire for control and predictability – Hopkins's title, *Scientific Advertising*, shrewdly plays to this, as does his opening paragraph. But more and more scientists and philosophers (though by no means all) now recognise

21

that throughout great territories of our experience this kind of certainty and control may be fundamentally impossible, and that the more we learn about these territories – the brain, the mind, the human sciences, chaos theory, quantum physics – the less certainty we can pretend to have.

A modern version of 'scientific advertising', then, would acknowledge that while there are certain aspects where patterns, regularities, and probabilities of cause and effect can be identified (such as the Ehrenberg-Bass work on patterns of purchasing behaviour), the major contribution of science to our understanding of advertising since the late twentieth century has been to reveal the importance of the subconscious, the complexity of human behaviour, the multivalent nature of communication – in short, to demonstrate that any dreams we might have had of reducing advertising to a set of rules or psychological principles that could be successfully applied by trained technicians, were illusory. This only leaves us feeling helpless if we assume that rational, logical process is the only way of getting things done. In fact, this kind of science invites us to return, with renewed confidence, to doing what all successful advertisers of the past did (including Hopkins) – to use their judgement, imagination, flair, brass neck, trial and error, and luck – in short, their humanity - as well as their intellect.

But after all that, this is not meant as a book about science either. I have written here predominantly about *practitioner* theories of advertising – the popular mental models that for the most part were created by people who worked in the business, and which have most influenced practice. There is also an extensive parallel universe of *academic* theory about how advertising works. This is not entirely irrelevant to the story I want to tell, and the history of academic theory would show both parallels to and connections with the history of practitioner theory (see Appendix 1). But to an extent that might surprise the outsider, the two worlds are in practice widely separate, despite some valiant attempts to build bridges between them, such as the work of Tim Ambler or Robert Heath. The vast majority of academics researching advertising in US universities have never worked in advertising; virtually no-one from an ad agency ever attends the Advertising Research Foundation (ARF) conference, or has ever even heard of ICORIA; hardly anyone who works in advertising ever reads even the most accessible of the academic journals on the subject. Whether this reflects more on the deplorable ignorance of advertising professionals, or the self-absorbtion of most advertising academics, is not a question I want to discuss here. But it means that a coherent narrative of advertising thought in practice can be presented without extensive reference to academic theory, and that is what I have set out to do.

My story, then, is about the advertising men and market researchers who have influenced advertising thinking and practice in the past century or so, and whose legacy still largely constructs the advertising culture of today. (And they *are* almost entirely men, and mostly Americans, with a few from the UK. I genuinely believe these patterns of gender and geography are part of the story, rather than any bias of mine; for more on the history of women in advertising agencies, see Fox, pp.284-299, and Marchand, pp.33-35.)

Part One, **Salesmanship**, outlines a family tree of advertising theories which derive from a common theme of rational persuasion. This is still in many ways the dominant or default model used by both advertisers and agencies, including creative departments, though as you will discover the basic principles have evolved over time into some radically differing and even contradictory shapes. It is remarkable how much of the everyday vocabulary of advertising comes from this tradition – a string of words including *proposition, benefit, reason why, message, attention, comprehension, conviction, impact,* and *recall,* which shape our thinking in ways we normally so take for granted we never notice it.

Part Two, **Seduction**, traces a parallel history of ideas about advertising which locate its effects less in rational persuasion and more in the power of images, symbols, emotions, and the subconscious mind. Such ideas are not new, though recent advances in psychology and neuroscience make them increasingly plausible. They nevertheless remain more controversial than the models of rational persuasion, partly because they are far harder to express in simple, logical terms, (and therefore to measure), and partly because they have sometimes been confounded with ethical questions.

As I wrote, it became clearer to me that each of these two models – rational persuasion and subconscious seduction – offers much that is of practical value, though equally each has some serious limitations*. It further seemed to me that despite the great historical importance of each of

---

* I use the phrase 'subconscious seduction' loosely in this book, to indicate a range of possible ways of thinking about advertising which are different from 'rational persuasion'. The phrase was first used (capitalised) by Dr.Robert Heath in his 2012 book, *Seducing the Subconscious,* to describe his own much more specific model of 'the psychology of emotional influence in advertising'. I should make it clear that while I much admire Robert's book (see Appendix 1), my use of the phrase is not identical with his.

these traditions, they aren't the only ways that it is possible to think about advertising. In Part Three, therefore, I begin by revisiting the subject matter of the first two sections in order to reflect more deeply on how each can be useful to us, and where each can be misleading or limiting. I then go on to identify four more ways of thinking about advertising, distinct from the first two. These are: advertising considered as simple **salience**, or fame; advertising considered as a means of creating and maintaining relationships, or **social connections**; advertising considered under the parallel but interestingly different theories that have characterised public relations, or **spin**; and finally, advertising considered simply as **showmanship**. (I don't make any great claim that these six different perspectives which I ended up with are an exhaustive list – others may well like to make a claim for more.) Each of these has its own history, and brings into our story some colourful characters who aren't always acknowledged in the advertising hall of fame, such as Edward Bernays and Phineas T. Barnum. Barnum, in particular, I found myself warming to more and more as I found out more about him, and his highly effective practice of what he himself called 'Humbug'; as I began to tire of wondering whether advertising should really be thought of as art or science, I inclined to think that perhaps, after all, we would be best to consider it as Humbug. Hence, at least, the title of the book.

*

This book has been brewing for maybe twenty years but its final emergence owes a lot to an invitation in the autumn of 2013 from Jim Carroll, Chairman of Bartle Bogle Hegarty

(BBH) in London, to give a series of lectures to the staff of his agency on 'the history of advertising thought' - a topic which he remembered hearing me talk about some years previously. Jim's request prompted me to look out material I hadn't visited for some time, including draft chapters from a long-abandoned book. The three lectures were well attended and the lively discussions that followed them both encouraged and helped me; indeed, the direction that the third lecture took owed a lot to the questions and comments of my BBH audiences. So I am grateful to Jim as the 'onlie begetter' of this text, also to him and his colleagues at BBH, especially Nick Kendall, for the way their contributions helped to shape the final outcome.

Although in the past I have normally illustrated lectures on advertising with examples of actual adverts, I took a decision early on that for these lectures I would do the opposite. This saved me the trouble of preparing visual aids, to be sure, but it also meant I had to rely on my own words to keep the audience engaged, so I'm not sure if it was the easy option or not. The more important reason I chose to do it this way was because I wanted people to focus on the universal relevance of the ideas I was presenting, and find their own examples to illustrate these, whether from history or from something they happened to be working on right now. It's an easy route to 'prove' a point you want to make about how advertising works, by choosing an ad that fits it neatly, and I've seen it done too often. (And ads, however interesting, usually 'date' rather quickly.)

Rightly or wrongly, I've tried to follow the same policy in this book; I do refer to a few ads to make specific points, but on the whole I've tried to avoid doing this, and I've chosen not to include any illustrations. I encourage you, if you're sufficiently interested, to apply any of the ideas here to your own choice of ads, from whatever source: there are plenty of historical ads from all periods available today online (The History of Advertising Trust is a good source of UK work), or in a variety of books such as the Taschen series of *All-American Ads*. Better still, try them on the ads you see tomorrow at the bus stop, on the TV, or on your Facebook page – and not least, on the campaigns you're working on yourself. If the ideas in this book have any validity, they should be applicable to any ads, in any medium, not just to a few chosen examples or the usual, fetishised, 'classics' (if I see that pregnant man again in a book about advertising I think I shall scream).

I hope you will find it a liberating experience.

Part One

Salesmanship

Advertising is selling, and the great
satisfaction of selling is closing the sale.
The advertising man can never close a sale;
in fact, he can never be certain that it was his
effort that made the sale possible.

Martin Mayer, *Madison Avenue USA,* p.39

Chapter One:

The Mountie Gets His Man

John E. Kennedy, AIDA, and the Reason Why.

One afternoon in the Spring of 1904, two men sat talking together in a comfortable office in the city of Chicago, high up on the corner of Wabash and Randolph. The elder of the two wore a wing collar, a watch on a heavy gold chain with an elk tooth fob, and a relaxed, superior manner. His name was Ambrose Thomas, and you might have taken him for a well-off retired broker or banker. The younger man, Albert Lasker, had a modern suit, dark wavy hair and an air of suppressed energy.

Thirty years after the great fire which destroyed most of the downtown area, Chicago was a booming city, the fourth largest in the world. Only one block away stood the Masonic Temple, at twenty two stories the tallest building in the world. Nearby, at State and Madison, more of the new 'skyscrapers' were rising around what was called 'the world's busiest corner'. Toward the South Side lay the huge expanse of the stockyards, where ever increasing numbers of immigrants from just about every European country were employed, in horrific conditions, to slaughter millions of pigs and steers for the whole United States. Chicago's position as the hub of the national railroad system made it the crossroads of the rapidly growing US economy. For the same reason, in the more salubrious air of the downtown 'Loop', the city was the centre of the nation's rapidly expanding advertising business.

Mr Thomas and Mr Lasker were the managing partners of advertising agency Lord and Thomas - the fastest growing agency in the US, and soon to overtake N.W.Ayer to become the largest. Its recent success owed everything to the drive and leadership of Albert Lasker, who had recently bought out the share of the eponymous Mr Lord on his retirement. Yet it was only six years since Lasker, in order to pay off a gambling debt, had joined the agency as an office boy. Today, a partner with an annual salary of $52,000, he was still only 23 years old.

The two men's conversation was interrupted by a knock, and a clerk entered with a note. Thomas glanced at it, pulled a face, and handed it to Lasker. The note was handwritten and read as follows: *'I am in the saloon downstairs, and I can tell you what advertising is. I know that you don't know. It will mean much to me to have you know what it is and it will mean much to you. If you wish to know what advertising is, send the word 'yes' down by messenger.'* It was signed, 'John E. Kennedy'.

Thomas was most disinclined to see this unknown man, but Lasker was intrigued: the stranger had offered to answer the question that was just then most on his mind. Although his own extraordinary energy and flair for organisation had already more than doubled the agency's billings, Lasker still worried endlessly about how he could define the principles that would make advertising more of a profession and less of a gamble. Was advertising 'news', as he had often been told? Was it 'keeping your name before the public' (as one of his competitors claimed)? He had pondered and discussed the question with many experienced people, but still lacked a convincing answer.

Kennedy's sheer nerve must also have appealed to Lasker, who was himself capable of similar effrontery. At the age of twelve he had founded a newspaper in his home town of Galveston, Texas, and personally solicited all the advertising for it. At nineteen, as a junior at Lord and Thomas, he had called without invitation on Mr Abe Rheinstrom of Rheinstrom's Brewery - at his home, in the middle of the day! - to pitch and win the account for the agency. So Lasker said, 'Let me see him. What have we got to lose?'.

A tall, muscular man in his late forties, with a flamboyantly curling moustache, was shown into Lasker's office. Lasker later described him as 'one of the handsomest men I ever saw in my life'. When he spoke, his accent was Canadian – he had been, among many other things, a member of the Canadian Mounted Police.

'Thank you for seeing me, Mr Lasker. I am sure you won't regret it. May I ask you first of all - what do *you* believe advertising is?'

'Well, Mr Kennedy, I am far from certain. But I believe it is to do with news.'

'No, sir. News is a technique of presentation, but advertising is a very different thing. I can give it to you in three words.'

'I am hungry. What are those three words?'

'Advertising is this: *Salesmanship in print.*'

The two men talked for an hour, after which they adjourned to the saloon downstairs, and went on talking until midnight. By that time, Lasker had already decided to offer Kennedy a job as head of copy.

What are we to make of this story? It presents itself as one of the foundation myths of modern advertising; in Lasker's own version, and the retelling by his biographer John Gunther (from which I in turn take my own), the episode is clearly intended as the moment when advertising emerged from the dark ages of muddle and superstition into the clear light of reason and accountability.

When I call it a myth, I do not mean that it never happened: I know of no reason to doubt the historical truth of the story. What I mean by a myth is a story that encodes, in a memorable form, deep beliefs about the way things are. In that sense, it seems to me, the story is a powerful myth.

Not only does the story *tell* us that 'advertising is salesmanship'. It also *shows* us, in a very particular way, what 'salesmanship' is. Kennedy has come to sell one thing, himself, to one person – Lasker. He knows that Lasker is the most powerful person in advertising. He believes he has something that Lasker needs and wants, his knowledge. His first challenge is to get in to see Lasker – to do this he has to get both his attention and his interest. His bold move of sending in a handwritten note gets the attention, and the words he uses – straight to the point – get Lasker's interest. Once he is inside, neither party wastes any time in small talk. Lasker indeed professes himself 'hungry' for the information Kennedy has promised. So Kennedy gives him the information – the main point first, and then goes on giving more and more information, until it is late in the evening . And the sale has been closed.

Selling had, itself, been dramatically systematised in the last decades of the nineteenth century. In 1887 John H. Patterson of National Cash Register introduced the first sales manual containing scripts for salesmen. One of his employees during this period was E. St Elmo Lewis, who later became head of advertising for Burroughs and in time a member of the Advertising Hall of Fame; it is Lewis who is generally credited with inventing the famous mnemonic AIDA – Attention, Interest, Desire, Action. (But see Dragon for a more nuanced history.)

Kennedy's pitch to Lasker demonstrates every phase of this formula. And when he says that advertising is 'salesmanship in print', he is introducing AIDA-type thinking to advertising. We may forget today that AIDA and its early variants were invented as models for personal selling, not for advertising. It was only as a result of equating advertising with selling that this, and the many related 'hierarchical models' that followed on from it, became commonly accepted as a natural description of advertising effects.

'What then', asked Lasker later that evening, 'is the secret of good salesmanship? What is it that actually *makes people buy*?'

'That too is simple', said the tall Canadian, drawing on his cigar. 'You have to give them a *reason why*.

'Imagine - if the proprietor of a grocery store should simply invite people to come in and buy, for no definite reason – he would get nowhere! But if he were to explain why his products are better – or why they are sold at a cheaper price yet are just as good as the other fellow's – if he could present *convincing arguments* to prove his superiority – then the chances are, like as not, people will flock to him.'

So after this evening, Lasker made Lord and Thomas into the home of 'reason why' advertising. He offered Kennedy a job as a copywriter. (He had some trouble obtaining approval for this hiring from Mr Thomas who had taken an unexplained dislike to Kennedy from the outset, but finally agreed 'on condition I don't ever have to see the fellow'.) Then, at Lasker's request, Kennedy taught him everything he knew about advertising. Every evening after work, they sat together discussing advertisements and how they could be improved.

At that time, the writing of copy was not regarded as a serious job in advertising agencies, who saw their role as brokers for the media. There was only one copywriter at Lord and Thomas – and he was paid $35 a week. But smart advertisers valued good copy, and would pay small fortunes to employ the best writers themselves. Kennedy at the time was working for Dr Shoop's Restorative, and to lure him away Lasker had to pay him $17,000 a year – a figure which would soon rise to $75,000. Lasker and Kennedy both saw that copy – the actual writing of advertisements – would in future become the most important way for an agency to create value for the client and their own competitive advantage. So Lasker moved some filing cabinets to create new office space, and began to hire and train journalists as copywriters. This was the beginning of modern copywriting practice.

Kennedy, despite his extrovert sales pitch to Lasker, turned out to be a morose and difficult character. He refused to teach the new copywriters because he found it difficult to talk to more than one person at a time, so Lasker himself took on this task. In 1907, after some perceived slight, Kennedy left the agency – he spent the rest of his life freelancing and doing various odd jobs, and died in 1928. But the ideas of 'salesmanship in print' and the 'reason why' continued to flourish at Lord and Thomas, soon under the guidance of an even more successful copywriter – Claude Hopkins.

Chapter Two:

The Great Majority of the Sane and Thrifty

Claude Hopkins and Scientific Advertising

In 1908 Albert Lasker was travelling by train to Philadelphia when he met an acquaintance, Cyrus Curtis, the proprietor of the *Saturday Evening Post*. Curtis said 'Lasker, I am just about to order a bottle of Schlitz beer as a result of an advertisement that I read, and you ought to go and get the man who wrote that advertisement'.

This was especially remarkable as Curtis was a virtual teetotaller who never allowed any advertising for alcoholic beverages in his own magazines.

The Schlitz advertisement had the headline 'Poor Beer vs. Pure Beer'. It was an excellent example of the 'reason why' philosophy that Kennedy had drummed into Lasker. It left the reader with the impression that to drink any beer other than Schlitz would be to court immediate disease from impurities, cheap ingredients, and fermentation.

Lasker discovered that the man who wrote the Schlitz ad was called Claude Hopkins. Hopkins was the son of a clergyman from Michigan, and had been brought up in considerable poverty in a strict nonconformist household. He had had to work for his living from the age of nine, first as a janitor in a church, later as a travelling lay preacher and then as a salesman for patent medicines. From these formative experiences he then moved into copywriting, which had made him extremely rich. 'You'll never get Hopkins by offering him money', a friend advised Lasker. 'But you *could* get him by offering to buy his wife an electric automobile.' This was surprising advice considering Hopkins's wealth, but his penurious upbringing had left him so incorrigibly mean that although an electric car was his wife's dream he could not bring himself to buy her one.

Lasker took Hopkins to lunch, and asked him if, 'as a token of his admiration', he might present his wife with an electric car. So Hopkins was won – admittedly, at a salary of $185,000 a year plus bonuses. He was to work for Lord and Thomas for the next eighteen years.

Shortly before his retirement in 1924, Claude Hopkins published a short book called *Scientific Advertising*. Although, as I mentioned earlier, it is not universally known today, it sold eight million copies and became an important influence on subsequent generations of advertising practitioners, including David Ogilvy and Rosser Reeves.

The title of *Scientific Advertising* echoes – no doubt deliberately – a bestselling management book from ten years earlier, Frederick W. Taylor's *Scientific Management*. Taylor was the original 'time and motion man'. He had discovered that by strict measurement and control of workers, managers could achieve major increases in productivity. 'Efficiency' was the management buzz word of the age. Hopkins cannily reflected this in the supreme confidence of his opening paragraphs, which are worth quoting again:

> The time has come when advertising has in some hands reached the status of a science. It is based on fixed principles and is reasonably exact. The causes and effects have been analysed until they are well understood. The correct methods of procedure have been proved and established. We know what is most effective, and we act on basic laws.
>
> Advertising, once a gamble, has thus become, under able direction, one of the safest of business ventures.

What were Hopkins's 'methods of procedure'? They build directly on the concepts of 'salesmanship in print' and the 'reason why', and may be summarised as follows:

1. An advertisement exists for no reason other than to sell. It should be evaluated by how many sales it makes.
2. A headline should 'hail a few people only' – those who are 'prospects waiting to buy'. It should not attempt to attract the attention of others.
3. Long copy sells. Use as many words, as many facts as possible. 'The more you tell, the more you sell'. Use smaller typefaces than editorial. Those who are interested in your product will read it; the others don't matter.
4. A good salesman is serious and respectable and gives information. He does not entertain, tell jokes, or 'wear

conspicuous clothes' (or, Hopkins says, 'the great majority of the sane and thrifty will despise him'). Humour has no place in advertising: 'People do not patronise a clown'.

5. Pictures should only be used because they can give information more concisely than words. They should never be used to attract attention or for decoration. White space, of course, is always wasted space.

It is interesting to compare Hopkins's rules with the advertising we see today in any newspaper or magazine, and especially with those which the ad industry celebrates in its own creative awards. These in particular appear not merely to ignore, but to deliberately contravene every one of Hopkins's recommendations. Cryptic headlines, bizarre visuals, and white space abound; copy of any sort is usually nowhere to be seen.

This raises an interesting series of questions. Was Hopkins wrong? Or are the modern copywriters and art directors wrong? Or should we just assume that the world has changed beyond recognition since 1923?

All these answers contain an element of truth, but none goes to the heart of the matter. Of course the world has changed a great deal, and you could argue that a lot of Hopkins's ads were aimed at a largely rural public, practical minded and short of money, who made more considered purchase decisions than perhaps many of us do nowadays. But we should always beware of thinking that people today are somehow more 'sophisticated' or 'ad-literate' than their great-grandfathers. There were, after all, many successful ads even before Hopkins which equally ignored his

THE ANATOMY OF HUMBUG

principles – advertisements for Pears' soap used art without copy (Millais's painting 'Bubbles') and humour (the filthy tramp writing a testimonial – 'Two years ago I used your soap, since when I have used no other').

In fact, even Hopkins's own practice was frequently at odds with the principles in *Scientific Advertising*. A few years before Lasker hired him, Hopkins was advertising manager for Swift and Co, a firm of Chicago packers. To launch Cotosuet (an inexpensive substitute for butter or lard), against a dominant competitor already in the market, Hopkins negotiated an alliance with Rothschilds, a large Chicago department store about to open new premises. He ordered from a baker *the largest cake in the world*, made from Cotosuet rather than butter. It stood, as high as the ceiling, filling an immense corner bay window at Rothschilds. The cake, in modern parlance, went viral. Police had to hold back the crowds. Over a hundred thousand people came to see the cake; many of them entered a 'guess the weight of the cake' competition, for which they had first to buy a pail of Cotosuet (Hopkins, pp.62-5). The sheer theatricality of this is quite different from the 'scientific', copy driven Hopkins we imagine from his best known book. (It also reminds us that early practitioners of 'advertising' had no qualms about considering events, promotions, sponsorship or PR as part of their trade.)

But when Hopkins wrote about 'advertising', he was basing his thinking on one specific model – what he called 'mail order' advertising, and what we today would more usually call 'direct response'. Hopkins's thinking may have been influenced by his early experiences in a travelling medicine show, but his espoused theories were based on what he had learnt from experience – from thousands of ads where he had been able to measure relative levels of coupon response.

Mail order ads are literally, 'salesmen' – each is a mechanism designed to close a sale, and its success in achieving this can be measured by counting the responses. At the most basic level, all that is required is for each coupon to carry a unique 'key number', so that each treatment, each insertion can be associated with its direct results. However there remain a number of variables in each case: not only the copy, but the publication, the position in the publication, and the day of the week. To attain a properly scientific evaluation of copy required a split run.

The first split run experiment was probably carried out before the end of the nineteenth century, and so by the time of Hopkins's book many thousands of such cases had been tried. The split run was based on the simple principle that newspapers or magazines were printed on multiple presses, two or more copies side by side. If the otherwise identical frames contained different advertisements, then every alternate copy would have the one or the other: a perfect experimental design. This enabled ad agencies to experiment with headlines, copy, visuals in endless detail until the response had been 'optimised'.

If you look at any newspaper or magazine today you will still find a great many ads that exist to close a sale. Today they will have a phone number or web address as well as a coupon, but the principle remains the same. And it is here that you will find, almost without exception, ads that obey Hopkins's rules. Headlines that eschew humour in order to hail a few people only: 'A real leather briefcase for only $39.99'; 'Do you suffer from painful piles?'. Plenty of factual copy, and pictures that illustrate the product. When it comes to selling off the page, experience continues to show, again and again, that Hopkins knew pretty much what he was talking about.

There is a great deal of power in this idea. It would seem strange otherwise that Hopkins became such an influential person in the history of advertising, and that he was so venerated by later agency leaders such as David Ogilvy and Rosser Reeves. In fact, the Hopkins model does not apply only to mail order advertising; it makes sense whenever there is a good story to be told, whenever the role of advertising is to 'hail a few people only', provide information, and close (or come close to closing) a sale. In my view, Hopkins is sadly under-valued by today's mainstream agency people, who appear to have abandoned the idea of *writing* advertisements altogether - and seem, too, to have lost the ability to write copy that anyone would read, let alone copy that sells. I needn't stress that this all has great relevance too when we consider the internet.

But where we can challenge Hopkins is on one big assumption he makes throughout *Scientific Advertising* – that all advertising is designed to work in this particular way. At one point he says quite explicitly, 'Advertising does not exist to keep your name before the people. It is not to help your other salesmen'. But why not?

In Part Two I will look more at the roles advertising can play that do not fit Hopkins's definition of a 'salesman'. But for the moment, let's notice the importance of these long past events to subsequent history and current practice.

What is the legacy today of Kennedy, Hopkins and indeed St Elmo Lewis? More than you might at first think. Their influence cannot be overestimated. Even though few people who work in advertising today may have heard of them, they introduced many of the key concepts in our textbook paradigms of advertising. Let me list them as follows.

1. **Attention**. The importance of 'attention getting' as the first stage in the process. We shall see in a moment how this idea was developed by Daniel Starch into something quite different from what Hopkins had in mind, and how it became even more influential in that form. Even today, and in media that were undreamt of in Hopkins's day, the concept of attention remains central to much advertising thinking: despite the fact that there has been for a long time convincing evidence that the quest for attention can often be mistaken and potentially damaging.

2. The idea that advertising always works by '**rational persuasion**', in other words, by the presentation of information and rational argument, in a form that is predominantly verbal. This idea too was to develop further, when it became linked to the importance of memory in advertising, but its influence is still there today whenever we talk in advertising about a *proposition*, a *benefit*, a *message*, or a *reason why*; it is

also evoked when we refer to ad executions as *'copy'*, or ask a question such as 'What are we trying to *say?*'. This remains our dominant mental model of advertising, so deeply encoded in our language and practice that it is hard to see it for what it is: one model among others, with its limitations as well as its uses, rather than a set of eternal truths.

3. At a deeper level still, *Scientific Advertising* created a powerful belief that good advertising could be defined in terms of Taylorian efficiency – that with enough measurement and experimentation, we could arrive at **rules** of what works best and progressively eliminate the trial and error and the wastefulness that either Lord Leverhulme or John Wanamaker (perhaps) lamented in their own advertising: 'I know half of my advertising budget is wasted, but no-one can tell me which half'. There is no evidence that either actually said this. But if either of them did, the irony is that each knew he owed much of his large fortune to advertising. Both men may have regretted they could not make their advertising more efficient – but neither would for a moment have considered reducing the sums he spent on it. In this, these two entrepreneurs differ from the risk averse mentality of many of today's marketers.

Advertising in its business context can be seen as a matter of inputs and outputs, of investments and returns, and much management thinking both then and now is programmed to look for ever increased efficiency. But this is also to suppose that advertising always works in ways that are predictable and analysable, that it can be subject to laws similar to those of engineering. This was, of course, Hopkins's promise, and no doubt the secret of his book's success – as a copywriter he had a talent for understanding and promising what his prospects wanted to hear. That opening paragraph is as calculated a come-on as Kennedy's tantalising note to Lasker.

But when Hopkins wrote, there was a great deal more confidence than there is today that the social or human sciences, then in their infancy as ideas, could with time approach to the simple certainties of Newtonian physics. The champion of this idea was Auguste Comte, the founder of 'positivism', who was still alive in Hopkins's day. Some people still persist in this belief, but as the twentieth century wore on more and more thinkers have come to question whether the two fields of study are at all comparable. People, both individually and in groups, seem to behave in ways that defy predictive analysis, no matter how much we study them and learn about them. (Meanwhile, even Newtonian physics itself has been called into question as Einstein and others have shown that Newton's formulas are predictive only within certain limitations.)

What if advertising is more like – well, let's leave 'art' aside for the moment, and say 'showbusiness'? What if there is no sure-fire formula for predicting a winner – and never will be? What if it depends less on calculation and more on individual inspiration, genius, and happenstance? These are hardly revolutionary thoughts in themselves, but the textbook paradigm has never really engaged with them beyond lip service. Such ideas do not lend themselves easily to traditional academic research, nor to the business world's emphasis on measurement and control. They do however make sense of a great deal that has happened, throughout its history, in the actual arena of commercial advertising. It may be that an excessive quest for efficiency has often been a constraining factor, rather than an enabling factor, in the production of effective brand communications.

Artistry, after all, was a crucial ingredient in the best mail order advertising too. In a speech given toward the end of his life, Bill Bernbach commented on a classic mail order ad from the twenties, 'They laughed when I sat down at the piano – but when I started to play – !' :

> What if this ad had been written in different language? Would it have been as effective? What if it had said, "They admired my piano playing", which also plays to the instinct of being admired? Would that have been enough? Or was it the talented, imaginative expression of the thought that did the job? That wonderful feeling of revenge. (Bernbach 1980)

If Hopkins had really been right in claiming that advertising was reducible to 'basic laws and procedures', there would have been no need for Lasker to pay him $300,000 a year – he could have trained any intelligent person to do the job. And so indeed could all his competitors. But Hopkins, presumably, did not write his book in order to give away trade secrets – he wrote it in order to advertise his agency, and demonstrate their superior understanding and reassure potential clients that they knew how to deliver 'efficiency'. The logical part he was happy to share, but the creative magic was the agency's own secret.

Chapter Three:

Passing Wind Loudly

Daniel Starch and the Quest for 'Attention'

It suited Hopkins, Lasker, and many other agency people to assert that all advertising must necessarily follow the same rules as mail order because that was where they had all the data, and where they felt confident they knew what the rules were. During the 1920s this became the dominant idea in advertising, and agencies vied with each other to produce books with titles like *Four Million Enquiries,* which showed off their credentials as mail order experts and elaborated more and more rules for advertising that would sell.

Not all the ads Hopkins wrote were, literally, mail order ads. But typically, even those that could not practically 'sell' off the page would include some kind of free offer for which the reader was invited to apply. The only reason for this was so that the agency could measure which copy was more effective in attracting response. It was not, of course, the same as a sale. But it was widely assumed that it would be an acceptable proxy for sales. It did at least indicate that the ad had been noticed and read.

And yet, if you look at print ads from the 1920s – for instance, Taschen's fat volume of 'All American Ads' from each decade – Hopkins's book begins to seem very odd indeed. Because here are many, many examples of ads depending on striking or amusing visuals; of short copy; of all sorts of practices Hopkins professed to disapprove of. These are not, for the most part, response ads – many are designed as poster or point of sale work – but even so, they demonstrate that many people commonly believed in their actual practice that there was much more to advertising than just 'salesmanship in print'.

However, the ideas of efficiency and 'scientific advertising' now had sufficient traction that other practitioners needed their own forms of response measurement if they were to compete with the mail order experts. The first man to create a successful business from this opportunity was a college professor called Daniel Starch.

Starch was born in Wisconsin, in an area with such a strong German immigrant heritage that he was to retain a slight German accent throughout his long life. In 1903, the year before Albert Lasker met John Kennedy, he graduated with a BA in psychology and mathematics – at 19, the youngest in his class. He took his MA in psychology and education at the University of Iowa, and after completing a PhD held a number of academic posts.

By 1923 he was a professor at Harvard Business School and was appointed by the American Association of Advertising Agencies (AAAA) as their head of advertising research. In that year - the same year as *Scientific Advertising* - Starch's own magnum opus, *Principles of Advertising*, was published. Starch repeats the definition of advertising as 'selling in print', but he expands on this in ways which differ from Hopkins. According to Starch, advertising fulfils the following roles in the selling process:

- it reduces sales resistance
- it develops a readiness to accept a product
- it creates a desire or demand for the commodity

All of these can be seen as embracing the idea of 'saleability' more than Hopkins did. Starch also defined five functions of advertising, based on his psychological theories, which formed the basis for much subsequent thinking:

- to secure attention
- to arouse interest
- to bring about conviction
- to produce action
- to impress the memory

Starch may not have meant these as an invariable sequence of events, but they have generally been interpreted as if they were because they so closely resemble the sequence of AIDA, which we met earlier. The one new element here introduced by Starch is memory. The addition of memory allows us conceptually to extend the AIDA selling model to situations where action cannot be taken immediately – the conviction must stay in the mind until the purchase situation presents itself. The implication is that even when advertising does not lead to an immediate sale, it works in the same way – there is merely a time lag between conviction and action which memory must make good.

Memory or recall was to become a major theme in subsequent advertising research and thinking, as we shall see later. However, Starch's biggest contribution to advertising practice has less to do with his writing and his theory than with the invention of a research technique that was to make him hugely wealthy. This was the recognition measure, more generally known as the Starch rating.

Starch and Associates was founded in Mamaroneck, New Jersey, in 1923, but it was not until 1937 that the company launched the process that was to make Starch a name on everyone's lips. Starting from the importance of 'attention' as the first step in successful advertising – without which the others were assumed to be impossible – Starch devised a simple and cheap method for measuring how many people reading a periodical had looked at each of the ads. Since the 1890s, advertisers had reasonably reliable data on how many people read each publication – but Starch suggested that the proportion of those whose attention was attracted by any particular ad might vary considerably. On Starch's model, if that proportion was low, it implied the ad was going to be less effective.

The method was simple. Readers were taken, page by page, through a publication they had read, and simply asked which ads they remembered looking at. As the results could easily be syndicated to every advertiser in the book, if necessary after the event, and as the publications themselves had an interest in subsidising the research too, the data could be sold very cheaply to lots of companies – advertising agencies themselves were often keen to buy the data to show to their clients, especially when the figures looked good.

The Starch rating became the prototype of commercially successful advertising research. Nothing in Starch's own theory justifies placing such total reliance on recognition as a measure of advertising success, but it was cheap, it was easy to understand, it was a universal currency, and it produced a single number. Something about the human psyche – perhaps especially the male psyche – loves the idea of comparing scores, league tables and rank orders. Its effect can be seen in many situations, from nations' obsession with Gross Domestic Product to Robert Parker's wine scores, and it appeals too in business. As soon as the Starch rating became available, everybody wanted to have a higher one than their competitors. Critics questioned, from the outset, whether a measure of recognition should be assumed to be a measure of selling effectiveness, but that was not a consideration that bothered many of the advertisers or the agencies who were buying the data.

Starch ratings still exist today, although they play a less dominant role than they did in the fifties and sixties. I used to have some publicity material from Roper Starch, the company who now sell the service, which only a few years ago claimed they could measure which execution 'pulls' better – cleverly using a word which ambiguously suggests both attracting attention and closing a sale. (As for the obvious metaphor of seduction, we'll return to that in Part Two.)

As Starch ratings quickly became popular, a debate developed between those advertising agencies who still believed in the 'mail order' school and those who were prepared to follow Starch. John Caples, a leading copywriter at BBDO – and the author of that famous direct response ad , 'They laughed when I sat down at the piano...' – was interviewed in 1955 by journalist Martin Mayer for his book *Madison Avenue USA*. If agencies want to get good Starch scores, said Caples,

> 'there's an easy way to beat that game. Instead of showing a big picture of the car, you show a big picture of Marilyn Monroe and a little picture of the car. If that doesn't work, you take some clothes off her' (p.249).

Other celebrated disciples of Claude Hopkins were similarly disparaging about getting attention for its own sake. Rosser Reeves, head of the Ted Bates agency and inventor of the 'Unique Selling Proposition' (USP), whom we shall meet shortly, remarked - 'You can always get attention by passing wind loudly at a party. But it may not do much for your social standing', while David Ogilvy claimed you could always get high attention by showing 'a gorilla in a jock strap'. Even Bill Bernbach argued that it would be wrong to attract attention by showing a man standing on his head, unless, for instance, you were advertising a product that would stop small change falling out of his pockets.

Leaving aside for a moment the real relevance of this measure, one thing is obvious: the type of ad you will write if you are aiming to maximise a Starch rating is, in just about every way, the exact *opposite* of what Claude Hopkins would have recommended. No longer are you 'hailing a few people only' – you want to attract the attention of *everyone* reading the periodical. To do this you will use every attention-getting trick you can think of – if not literally the gorilla in a jock strap, you will want large pictures, unusual visuals, cryptic headlines, all those things that were anathema in *Scientific Advertising*. Clowns in conspicuous clothes? – bring them on!

The way these two simple models totally contradict each other begins to explain a common unresolved conflict which bubbles away in so many advertising planning meetings. Those who place a high priority on maximising attention as a goal will argue for the white space and the eye catching visual, while those who believe in the power of information continue to push for facts and long copy. Others tie themselves in knots by trying to have it both ways at once. But typically, no-one realises that they are unconsciously arguing to a script written some eighty years ago by people they have probably never even heard of.

And who is right? Well, that will certainly depend on the circumstances. But more importantly, we could be aware that there are many ways in which advertising can be effective, and that neither the constructs of *information* or *attention* in themselves are necessarily the most useful or important. Much successful advertising contains no information, and much also works without maximising conscious attention as measured by Starch or by recall techniques. The question is not so much to rule in favour of Starch or Hopkins, but to take a big step back and consider what other ways there are of imagining the ways advertising works – which we will consider in Parts Two and Three of this book.

Chapter Four:

Get This Into Your Head

Rosser Reeves and Message Recall

eanwhile, let's return to another key concept which grew in importance in advertising thinking during the middle decades of the last century – the concept of memory, or recall.

I mentioned that Starch had raised the idea of 'impressing the memory' as one of his five key roles of advertising. Memory, only a few decades earlier, had been one of the first topics to interest the infant science of psychology, and scientists such as Ebbinghaus had conducted experiments into how many nonsense syllables people could memorise. In Hopkins's book, memory played a relatively small part, because his concept of an advertisement, as we have seen, was a device for selling there and then. But as agencies engaged themselves more consciously with the idea of an unspecified time lag between exposure to the advert and buying behaviour, memory took on more importance in advertising theory and research.

Starch's own recognition method, to be sure, involved an aspect of memory, but what it really set out to measure was attention – if anything, it assumed that the respondent's memory was perfect and that what they claimed to have noticed was an accurate recollection of their experience while reading. We now know – better than Starch did – that the human capacity for recognition is extremely high and surprisingly accurate. Nevertheless, there are reasons to suppose that in the kind of test situation Starch used there was considerable room for misclaiming. People might well have seen an ad before, but in a different magazine or a longer time ago. They might be responding to elements of an ad rather than the ad as a whole. And they might also be self censoring, consciously or otherwise, what they admitted to have caught their attention.

A younger contemporary of Starch and also an academic, George Gallup had had plenty of experience of this last sort of bias. For his doctoral dissertation at the University of Iowa, he had carried out a readership study of the *Des Moines Register and Tribune*. 'The question was, what did people read?' (as Gallup described his work, many years later) 'Well, you ask them and they say, the editorials and the national news, never the comics or the sports.' At that time Gallup himself had used a reading and noting approach, similar to that of Starch, to overcome the problem.

Then in 1932 Raymond Rubicam, of Young and Rubicam, hired the bright young mid-westerner to head up the first proper ad agency research department. Gallup continued to work with Y&R until 1947, when he left to concentrate on his own company which he had founded in 1935, the American Institute of Public Opinion. Gallup's name is still best known today among the general public as the founder of the opinion poll, and sprang to prominence when he predicted accurately the election of Franklin Roosevelt in 1936.

It was therefore with an impressive track record in the ability to predict results that Gallup and Robinson, in 1951, launched their own ad testing system – called simply, and significantly - *Impact.* They promised to advertisers – they only sold to advertisers, never to agencies – a system that they argued would be both more reliable and more diagnostic than the familiar Starch rating.

Gallup's methodology differed from Starch in that it did not take readers through a magazine, but asked them which ads they remembered seeing in it. For each ad that was recalled (prompted or unprompted), the respondent was also asked to remember what the ad was saying.

Thus the concepts of recall and message recall were introduced, which, like attention, have occupied a central role in advertising research – and advertising thinking - ever since.

The 1950s saw the growing importance of television, and the centre of the advertising world had now shifted from Chicago to New York. It was a time of enormous energy, inventiveness and intellectual ferment in advertising, far more than that excellent drama *Mad Men* really shows, which is why Martin Mayer's 1958 book *Madison Avenue USA* remains for me perhaps still the most valuable single book on advertising. (I would also recommend Stephen Fox's great history of American advertising, *The Mirror Men.*) While the old school of evaluation by coupon response was fighting a rearguard battle – and would eventually live on in a separate world of 'direct response', familiar to us today – the new orthodoxy now emerging in advertising evaluation was in the form of survey research, measures of awareness, message recall, and attitudes. This new orthodoxy built on the work of Starch and Gallup, but also continued to rest on some deep foundations inherited from Hopkins and Kennedy – the central idea of information or message transmission, the importance of the 'reason why', and the various 'hierarchy of effects' models which originated with AIDA. It is important to understand this worldview, because it remains substantially the one that still dominates advertising research and practice today. I will illustrate it by referring to two key books, both very influential, and both published in 1961.

The first was written by a management consultant, Russell Colley, in response to a brief from the Association of National Advertisers in the US. The ANA, not unreasonably, posed a series of questions to Colley which are all about how much to spend on advertising and how to allocate that spending: questions which still concern any advertiser today. Colley provides no direct answers to such questions. He asserts that it is not possible to relate advertising to financial outcomes in any meaningful way. He applies, instead, the then fashionable theory of 'management by objectives', and his measurable objectives are all set in terms of survey research questions – brand awareness, advertising awareness, message recall, claimed usership, brand attitudes. Colley's book is called *Defining Advertising Goals for Measured Advertising Results* - this unwieldy title fortunately acronyms to DAGMAR, who it seems was a popular pin up girl at the time. It's not such a stupid book as it's sometimes held to be, and frankly a good deal more thoughtful than many of today's off the peg 'tracking studies', but its fundamental flaw is that it fails to see how the move from sales based outcomes to survey based outcomes inevitably requires making assumptions about how advertising works – and Colley largely takes over the hierarchical, 'salesmanship' models that were already established. Chapter 13, for example, is called 'What's the Message?'; and later on DAGMAR's own version of AIDA appears, slightly but significantly altered:

Unawareness - Awareness – Comprehension – Conviction – Action

Here 'Attention' – paid to the ad – has been replaced by 'Awareness' – of the product. In fact, many people today think that the first A in AIDA stands for Awareness, and assume it refers to awareness of the advertising: all part of the retrospective justification of ad awareness as a measure. The DAGMAR model further asserts that advertising must be understood and believed before it can be acted on, both questionable assumptions that have continued to bedevil advertising and ad research ever since.

The second book, which has been perhaps even more influential, is *Reality in Advertising* by Rosser Reeves. Reeves was the head of the Ted Bates agency which became hugely successful under his leadership, either despite or because of the fact that the ads they produced were notoriously formulaic and irritating. Reeves was a fascinating man, highly intelligent, a published poet and author of a book on shooting pool that is still apparently a classic in its field. When it came to advertising his strength lay in having a very clear and simple set of beliefs about how to do it, and the ability to communicate these to his clients. Like Hopkins, he wrote clear, brutally simple copy and his book's success owes a lot to his prose style.

Reeves is firmly in the tradition of 'advertising as salesmanship'. He was a fan of Hopkins and refers to him often; he also repeats with approval the story of Lasker's meeting with Kennedy. He borrows from both the idea that advertising is a form of selling, and that selling is primarily about information. Where he adapts Hopkins, is in shifting away from the 'more you tell, more you sell' long copy of the direct response ad, to arguing for a single, simple sales message that can be lodged in the memory. Reeves called this, memorably, the Unique Selling Proposition. The USP, to be clear, only needed to be 'unique' in so far as you were the only brand to claim it – Reeves acknowledged that most competing products didn't really differ. Examples he gives are Hopkins's own 'washed in live steam' (all beer bottles are), and 'gets rid of film on teeth' – 'so, indeed, does every toothpaste'.

Reeves asserted that

the consumer tends to remember just one thing from an advertisement – one strong claim, or one strong concept.(p.34)

He produced no real evidence for this claim – and I know of none myself to support it – but it has been so often repeated ever since that it now seems to be universally believed, not least in creative departments. Reeves argued therefore that successful advertising should be focused on a single, strong claim or proposition, and lodge this in the consumer's memory. Hence his new definition of advertising, which he offered as an updating of 'Salesmanship in Print':

ADVERTISING IS THE ART OF GETTING
A UNIQUE SELLING PROPOSITION
INTO THE HEADS OF THE MOST
PEOPLE AT THE LOWEST
POSSIBLE COST

(p.121)

The violent, invasive nature of the metaphor in this says a lot about Reeves's approach. He was not interested in charming consumers, or whether they liked the advertising – all that mattered was that the USP could be hammered into their heads.

It would be very difficult, at this remove, to know whether Reeves's campaigns were as effective as he claimed. Tim Broadbent, a great admirer of Reeves, has explored the Bates archives and tells me that no data survive from this period. Certainly Reeves was doing something right, and his clients approved of it. Whether it was what he claimed is another matter, and I will explain later why I think it doubtful that Reeves's campaigns really exemplified his theory of the USP. Nevertheless, it would be hard to overestimate the influence that Reeves's idea of the Unique Selling Proposition has had on both agencies and clients to the present day; even, paradoxically, among creative departments who would regard Reeves's own work with deep contempt. It survives in the popularity of the word 'proposition' itself, and in the structure of virtually all creative briefing forms which centre on 'the single most important thing we want to say'. (And that word '*say*', with its emphasis on something that can be put into words, is also significant.) It's supported in textbooks and advertising courses - a student website points out, as one example, that even today ' in creative portfolio classes at the University of Texas at Austin, students are instructed to find one main point to feature as a selling point with their ads'. Reeves's emphasis on 'the single-minded proposition' in a successful ad is perhaps the most commonly and deeply held belief in agencies – despite the fact that it is based on no real evidence, nor even on a coherent theory. Even to question it is, I have discovered, often regarded as heresy.

I will come back to Reeves again in Part Two, because he also needs to be understood in the context of other things that were happening in the fifties and sixties, the era of *Mad Men* and so-called 'motivation research'.

To end Part One, I will briefly review the ideas presented so far. From Kennedy and Lasker, Hopkins, Starch, Gallup, and Reeves, the advertising business has inherited a range of ideas all based on the fundamental concept of advertising as a form of selling, or in the old word, 'salesmanship'. Much of the language that we take totally for granted in advertising practice, we owe to one or other of these practitioners: the **proposition**, the **message**, the **reason why**, **impact**, **attention**, **awareness, recall.** There are certain assumptions that all these theories share – that selling requires conscious attention, that it involves a process of rational **persuasion, comprehension, conviction**, and the transmission and memory of predominantly verbal information. These assumptions still underlie much of our current discourse about advertising, even though, as we shall see, they can be strongly challenged. At the same time, theories based on selling have been used to justify some radically opposed practices – both long copy and single messages, both advertising that 'hails a few prospects only' and advertising which is expected to achieve mass attention, both advertising that is intended to trigger immediate response and advertising which is expected to lodge a verbal message in the memory. This indigestible smorgasbord of contradictory beliefs still gives rise daily to unresolved conflicts within agencies, or between agency and client, when designing campaigns.

But there have, from the very earliest times, been alternative ways of thinking about advertising based on very different assumptions: alternatives which have generally been practised in fact even if not legitimised in theory. In the next part of the book I will explore the most important of these, and consider how much successful advertising has always worked through means other than rational persuasion or verbal messages, and has achieved business success without seeing itself as a tool for selling.

Part Two:

Seduction

Se pourrait-il que séduire fasse si peur (la séduction est depuis toujours considerée comme l'arme du démon, un moyen diabolique...) que les chercheurs en publicité n'aient jamais voulu l'inclure dans le champ de leurs études?

[Could it be that the idea of seducing is so frightening (seduction has always been considered the work of the devil, an evil technique...) that advertising researchers have never wanted to include it in their field of study?]

Claude Bonnange and Chantal Thomas,
Don Juan ou Pavlov, p.55

Chapter Five:

Across the Street from Freud

Ernest Dichter and Motivation Research

As a teenager growing up in Vienna in the nineteen-twenties, Ernest Dichter would go once a week with his brothers and his father ('a spectacularly unsuccessful salesman') to the *Tröpferlbad* or public showers. For a sensitive and introspective young man, the experience evoked contradictory feelings, both connected with his Jewishness. On the one hand, the Sabbath eve ablutions had a powerful symbolic force: he 'not only washed away all the physical dirt, but all the moral dirt accumulated during the week', and this sense of renewal was reinforced by the weekly change of clothes that followed. At the same time, it could be a painful and embarrassing experience. With his red hair, Dichter was not generally recognised as a Jew in the anti-Semitic climate of pre-war Vienna. In the public showers, however, his race was frequently the occasion of unpleasant remarks.

Dichter's first job was as a window dresser in his uncle's department store in Vienna. Then, against his father's wishes, he took himself in 1929 to Paris to study at the Sorbonne. A chance encounter with a pretty girl (he was always to remain susceptible to such meetings) induced him to change his course from art to psychology. Returning to Vienna, he gained his doctorate in 1934, and then began to practice as a psychoanalyst. As the prospect of a Nazi *anschluss* became more likely, he decided with his wife to leave Austria, and applied for an American visa. Against the odds, he managed to convince the US Vice Consul that his psychoanalytic skills would be of unique benefit to the United States:

> My argument used with Mr. Thompson was new and surprising: that one can not simply ask people why they are doing the things they do, but that one has to use depth psychology to find these things out. Many of these problems cry out for solutions. But first we have to find the real reasons for the actions of people... We are afraid to recognise that a majority of our decisions concerning trivial or important matters are governed by emotions which are not always easy to recognise. At all costs, we want to retain the illusion that we are guided by rational factors. (Dichter, p.24)

Dichter displayed in that meeting the talent for salesmanship that had always eluded his father. He proposed that his 'motivational research' could address such issues as criminality, productivity, strikes, vandalism... 'I have been trained' he told the vice consul, 'to draw people out, to find out what really makes them tick.' The official was sold. He sent a personal affidavit of support to Washington, and as a result the Dichters sailed for New York in September 1938.

They arrived with no money. Dichter took a modest job at a small market research agency, where despite a friendly relationship, his boss was too frightened to make use of his new ideas. So Dichter wrote a promotional letter for himself to six companies:

'I am a young psychologist from Vienna and I have some interesting new ideas which can help you be more successful, effective, sell more and communicate better with your potential clients'. (Dichter, p.33)

He had four replies: one was from the Compton ad agency, who wanted him to advise them on Ivory soap. Dichter took what he described as a *gestalt* approach to the problem – the field of study was not soap, but bathing. He carried out a series of interviews with young men and women at the YMCA about their bathing habits:

I found out that the Saturday night bath was still a very important ritual... The young girls told me, very innocently, that before they went out on a date, they bathed in a particularly careful fashion. When I was curious they said, 'Well, you never can tell...'. I found out that such things as lathering oneself completely and then letting the shower water gradually take off the lather from one's body, was not only pleasant, but had some very peculiar undertones of undressing and erotic pleasure....The result was an advertising campaign, 'Be smart and get a fresh start with Ivory Soap'. (Dichter, p.35)

Another of Dichter's first clients was the Chrysler Corporation, who brought him to Detroit to revive the stalled sales of the Plymouth range. Dichter's big idea for this project was to recognise the importance of the convertible in the range. Though typically only 2% of sales, a convertible attracted many more viewers in the car showroom. Dichter hypothesised the symbolic significance of the convertible, especially to older men, as 'youth – the wind blows through your hair....Many men have a secret wish for a mistress... Buying a convertible represents the realization of this wish.... Of course, most bought the sedan, the "wife", comfortable and safe. The convertible, the "mistress", youthful, was the dreamer. It was psychologically desirable and effective, therefore, to use a convertible as the sales attraction, the "bait".'

This story, now well known, was picked up by *Time* magazine and quickly made Dichter famous ('Viennese Psychologist Discovers Gold Mine for Chrysler Corporation'). It was 1940 and he was still only 33 years old. He went on to work for a huge number of agencies and advertisers, at first as an independent consultant, then in 1953 founding the Institute for Motivational Research in a curious, castle-like house in the small town of Croton on Hudson outside New York City.

Dichter was only one of a number of researchers, with backgrounds in sociology or psychology, who left Europe under similar circumstances and who were to have a powerful influence on advertising thinking and research in the 1950s – these included Paul Lazarsfeld and his wife Herta Herzog, and Alfred Politz. But Dichter was probably the most famous and flamboyant practitioner of what became known as 'motivation research' (MR) – as well as being, without much doubt, the most imaginative and least rigorous researcher. Dichter's strengths were a constantly creative imagination, an ability to look at things in new ways, and to use his own introspections as a jumping off point for new ideas (as the weekly visit to the *Tröpferlbad* was happily recycled for Ivory Soap). How much he really used his research data, or classic psychoanalytic techniques, is more doubtful.

He also had a considerable flair, as we have already seen, for self publicity, and the association of his name with Freud did a great deal to legitimise his practice in the US – even though the closest connection he ever had with the founder of psychoanalysis was probably when, as a student, Dichter lived just across the street from him in Berggasse.

The main idea Dichter borrowed from Freud was that people's own motivations and reasons for their actions are normally unknown to themselves, and their own explanations of their behaviour are just empty post-rationalisations. The 'real' motives, which Dichter would offer with more plausible advocacy than proof, would be based on such emotional drives as security, status, and quite frequently, as in our two examples, sex.

Dichter also took for granted the power of symbolism, how one thing can stand for another, and his interpretations of visual patterns, such as the radiator of the Ford Edsel, anticipate some of the later work of semioticians. And he was influenced by the theory of *gestalt*, of seeing the whole pattern or context together rather than as a set of separable perceptions. He claimed that he invented the use of the word 'image', as in 'brand image', in 1940, as an attempt to translate the sense of *gestalt* into English. Dichter further explained this as 'the totality, the melody. The melody is more than individual notes.' (Dichter, p.35)

Many people in Dichter's lifetime described him as essentially a brilliant copywriter or ideas man by another name, and Martin Mayer even compared him to Claude Hopkins. But what differentiated Dichter from Hopkins or other successful copywriters was not so much the output from his process, as the underlying theory that he articulated for how he did it. There is little real distance between Hopkins's intuitive association of sex with shampoo in 'Hair that you love to touch', and Dichter's steamy eroticising of Ivory Soap. But there is all the difference in the world between Hopkins's description of the buyer as a rational, conscious weigher-up of product benefits, and Dichter's suggestion that we are driven by obscure emotional forces of which we remain in ignorance. As often in the history of advertising, the espoused theories are miles apart, while the theory in action could be the same.

The idea of 'motivation research' quickly caught on, and the name was used in association with a number of other researchers, some of whom saw themselves as very different in their approach from Dichter. At the opposite extreme, Alfred Politz – a German émigré with a background in mathematics and physics – was a great deal more rigorous in everything he did than Dichter ever was. (One consequence of this was that a Politz study was usually so expensive that only the biggest corporations could afford it.) He was also sceptical of Dichter's populist assumption that there was somehow one 'real motive' behind any aspect of behaviour. Nevertheless, he and Dichter also had some things in common. Both, for instance, began any research project with conscious introspection to generate hypotheses, and both would put considerable emphasis on qualitative research to develop these further. The differences became more apparent in the rigorously piloted and sampled quantitative surveys which Politz regarded as all important, but which for Dichter were apparently dispensable.

Other famous names in the MR movement included Louis Cheskin and James A. Vicary. Cheskin ran the Color Research Institute, which applied theories of subconscious motivation to pack design: working alongside Leo Burnett, Cheskin was instrumental in the famous 1956 relaunch of Marlboro. Marlboro, being a filter tipped cigarette, was originally positioned as a women's brand, but in the wake of the first major evidence linking smoking to lung cancer, the intention was to re-design the brand to appeal to men. Cheskin proposed the strong red colour and the chevron device, which he believed would subconsciously evoke the image of a medal and thus heroic masculinity. The concept of the 'brand image' was becoming accepted around this time, and its respectability can be specifically dated to a 1955 article in *Harvard Business Review*, 'The Product and the Brand', by Burleigh Gardner and Sidney Levy (two more academic sociologists who had found a rewarding new career in the booming world of advertising.)

James A. Vicary claimed academic credentials, though

it is now doubted whether he really did have the PhD he pretended to. Tall and good looking, he also showed considerable flair for publicising himself and his business. One of his early experiments, still quite famous today, involved monitoring the eye-blink rates of people walking round supermarkets: as they cruised the aisles the blink rates dropped to half of normal, which Vicary described as 'trance-like' – they then accelerated to higher than normal as the time came to pay, indicating stress. But he was to become most famous for his experiment with 'subliminal advertising'. In 1956 Vicary installed a tachistoscope in a cinema in Fort Lee, NJ, which projected the verbal messages 'Drink Coke' and 'Eat Popcorn' on the screen for 1/30,000 of a second. Vicary hypothesised that while this was far too quick to register consciously, it would be subconsciously noticed and could influence behaviour; and indeed, on the alternate days that the subliminal messages were projected, sales of Coke and popcorn rose enormously. This experiment was widely publicised, and caused huge alarm. If it was so easy to brainwash people without their knowledge, what else might this technique be used for in the wrong hands? (Recall that this was the McCarthy era, when the American public were highly concerned about the 'communist threat'.) The US, the UK, and other governments rushed through legislation banning 'subliminal advertising'. And as we shall see, the alarm caused by Vicary's stunt made a major contribution to the eventual reaction against motivation research as a whole.

But in fact, a stunt is all that it was. After the hysteria had died down a bit, scientists who attempted to replicate Vicary's results found that these kind of message exposures had no effect at all on behaviour. Eventually, someone thought to drive over the George Washington Bridge and visit Fort Lee. It turned out the cinema manager had never heard of Vicary, had never installed a tachistoscope, and indeed the cinema was too small for the numbers claimed in Vicary's report. In 1962 Vicary admitted that the whole thing had been a hoax designed to prop up his business (Robinson, pp.16-20). A widespread fear of 'subliminal advertising' has however persisted to this day.

Nevertheless, the more solidly grounded theories of the motivation researchers – the importance of subconscious motivations, of associations, of emotions, of visual symbolism, etc – had immense relevance for advertising. The man who most clearly spelled this out was a social researcher working for the *Chicago Tribune*, Pierre Martineau, who published in 1957 a book which he called *Motivation in Advertising*. Martineau starts from an obvious place: he looks at actual advertisements, and observes that

modern advertising is not just a posting of claims, a bare-bones statement of fact. It is far, far, from being just a reliance on words and logic. It is rather a fusion of many modes of human communications, including language. Advertising as we know it today uses layout and illustration, both photography and art; it uses color and music, even choreography and drama. Actually it also uses language in a far more expressive way than just to present rational thought. Any given ad may have any number of appeals which are not openly presented. It may have esthetic appeal, entertainment value, or irrelevant but highly valuable information, as well as various psychological attractions. Besides economic self-interest, advertising leans heavily on such other psychological processes as suggestion, association, repetition, identification, fantasy, etc. ... so much more is going on than just a sales argument with the consumer. (p.13)

Martineau stresses, again and again, how advertising uses visual symbolism and connotative language to create emotional associations. Such associations relate to the deeper emotional motivations of the consumer. 'People... are changeable, suggestible, highly non-rational, motivated far more by emotion and habit and unconscious causes than by reason and logic.' (p.28)

Coming to such ideas from the simple orthodoxies of Rosser Reeves, we may be struck by how 'modern' they seem; we may also wonder why only recently we appear to have rediscovered similar ideas about the importance of the subconscious and the symbolic. So whatever happened to 'motivation research'? I think there is a story here, and it's an important one in our history of advertising thinking.

Chapter Six:

The Bare and Pitiless Sunlight

The Strange Death of Motivation Research.

Why did 'motivation research' apparently vanish sometime around 1960? I am going to start my inquiry by referencing Harry Henry's 1958 book, *Motivation Research*. Henry was a British researcher who later became editor of *Admap*, and the fact this book exists incidentally tells us that MR was a phenomenon in the UK as well as in the US. Henry was a rigorous researcher and by no means a Dichter-like intuitive, so his book also shows us how MR was not separate from the mainstream tradition of market research – rather like 'neuroscience' today, it was probably seen by many as the way of the future. Which again makes it more interesting to ask why it disappeared so suddenly.

At the very end of the book, Henry acknowledges that MR has attracted a lot of controversy, which he categorises under three headings:

1. Those advertising and marketing people who are anti-any kind of research, preferring to rely on their own judgment and intuition. Henry is rather dismissive about this group, calling them the 'obscurantists... since

they are swimming against the tide of business practice in general too much attention need not be paid to them' (p.215). But then Henry was himself a researcher with his own bias. In fact, the rejecters of research have continued to be with us, and in some areas have become more vociferous.

2. The more traditional school of researchers, who based their work on the assumption that consumer decision making was relatively rational and transparent, and could be accessed through conscious questioning in survey research.

3. An ethical or moral challenge to the idea that people can be manipulated against their will by studying what goes on in their subconscious.

These three points of view, we may notice in passing, are all radically opposed to each other. The third assumes that MR works, indeed is frighteningly powerful as a technique – if it were hokum it would hardly raise any ethical concerns, beyond perhaps an accusation of fooling its clients. The first two argue that MR is quite unnecessary, but are themselves directly opposed, being pro- and anti- research in general.

So, as in a good murder mystery, we can take Henry's three critical groups as three very different suspects, each with their different motives for doing away with motivation research. Let us examine each of them further.

1. The anti-research brigade.

Certainly some of the rejecters of research would just have been very old school – the Roger Sterlings of the ad business. But during the fifties, acceptance of research in advertising was widespread in most agencies. Famous campaigns such as Marlboro and Esso were helped by research. Top researchers worked for big agencies: Gallup for Y&R, Herta Herzog at McCann's, and David Ogilvy spoke out for its importance. It took a certain bravery to publicly argue against research.

However, argue against it is just what one influential group did – the agencies that were soon to be identified with the 'creative revolution' in one important narrative of advertising history. The pioneer of this movement was Bill Bernbach. In 1947, while creative director at Grey, Bernbach had written:

> There are a lot of great technicians in advertising. And unfortunately they talk the best game. They know all the rules... They can give you fact after fact after fact.... But there's one little rub. Advertising is fundamentally persuasion, and persuasion happens to be not a science, but an art. (*The original letter is reproduced in Cracknell, p.11*)

Soon afterwards, Bernbach started his own agency, Doyle Dane Bernbach (DDB), which rapidly became famous for its bold, irreverent and frequently humorous campaigns. Bernbach based its work on clear principles: respect the audience, be original, speak to people in their own language, trust your judgment. Research, whether motivational or more traditional, played no part in this. Without the authority of research to guide decision making, the agency leaders asserted their own authority as experts, it being a condition of business that any client agreed in advance to go with the agency's recommendation. (Looked at another way, you could also see their rejection of research as an attempt to discredit any alternative source of authority in the decision process.)

Bernbach's stance has been much admired, envied, and in a few significant instances emulated by other agencies, especially in the creative departments. The second generation of 'creative' agency was spearheaded by Papert Koenig Lois (PKL), who replaced Bernbach's laid-back, gentlemanly brand of arrogance with a much more confrontational, street-fighting style. This was followed in the USA by Carl Ally and others, and soon picked up in the UK by Collett Dickenson Pearce (CDP) under the leadership of Colin Millward and John Pearce, and later Frank Lowe. All these agencies produced highly influential work which other creative departments aspired to copy, and their rejection of research accordingly became a widespread article of faith among creative people – despite the fact that many of them were not in a position to avoid it.

I believe this was an important development in the history of advertising practice. However, hardline creative-led agencies like PKL and CDP have always been a small though high profile minority – and most clients continued to place great reliance on research, and obliged their agencies to put up with it. So although Bernbach and his successors may have had strong motives for seeing MR disappear, I don't believe they had the power to have got rid of it.

2. The Traditional Researchers.

It would be misleading to suggest that there was any clear division between 'traditional' and 'motivation' researchers in the 1950s. There was a broad spectrum of approaches and the best researchers were quite eclectic, attempting to synthesise new psychoanalytic concepts with the scientific rigour of well-conducted survey research. (The best work anticipates things that are only now being developed in the field of 'implicit research'.) Such people included Alfred Politz, Paul Lazarsfeld, Herta Herzog, Louis Cheskin, and Harry Henry. Ernest Dichter, as we have seen, lay towards one extreme, high on intuition and low on scientific rigour – in reality, much closer to a man like Bernbach than you might think (though that was also exactly why they might see each other as rivals). At the other end of the spectrum, we must consider long established and lucrative techniques such as those of Gallup and Starch, and a wider body of survey research asking straightforward questions about opinions and attitudes in ways that pre-dated (and would survive) motivation research – very much as described in Russell Colley's *DAGMAR*.

Within this more complex situation, there would have been rivalries, and there was certainly plenty of room for controversy about the validity of different techniques and assumptions (Henry's closing chapter gives a very nuanced overview of these). But on the whole, the growth of motivation research was good for the research industry as a whole. It created lots of opportunities for academics to get well paid jobs, and – although many researchers resented Dichter's self publicising – it made research, for once, a bit sexy. Left to their own devices, the research establishment would I think have continued to integrate the new approaches with their established skills, as Harry Henry's book suggests. But what in fact happened, after motivation research became a dirty word, was a progressive narrowing of market research, an increasingly dogmatic reliance on limited techniques, a lack of experimentation or new thought, and in practice, more and more sloppy and bastardised versions of techniques pioneered by earlier, more inventive researchers.

So I don't believe it was the other researchers who did for MR.

3. The Ethical Attack.

In the same year as *Motivation in Advertising*, and a year before *Madison Avenue USA*, a third new book by a journalist appeared - which had a far greater impact, sending ripples far outside Madison Avenue itself. This was *The Hidden Persuaders* by Vance Packard.

While Martin Mayer's *Madison Avenue USA* took an attitude of detached fascination to its subject, Packard's book was firmly in the tradition of American 'muckraking' journalism. His thesis was that 'techniques of mass persuasion through the subconscious' posed a deep threat to democracy and freedom. Using the more extravagant claims of 'motivational researchers' such as Dichter, Cheskin and Martineau, Packard claimed that advertising was developing sinister scientific techniques to manipulate beliefs and behaviour without people even being aware of it, culminating in the prospect that these techniques could be used in the political arena as well as in commercial selling.

Advertising people have usually been rather furious with Packard, in a way that suggests that for all his unfairness, he touched a nerve. Winston Fletcher, in his admirable history of advertising in the UK, *Powers of Persuasion*, claims that *Hidden Persuaders* has nothing to do with advertising, being a book about research, and generally bogus research at that – thus distancing the ad industry from Packard's accusations. With respect to Winston's shade, I think this is disingenuous. Yes, Packard is unfair, in that he cleverly strings together things that are factual but often innocent, a good deal of innuendo, and some genuinely alarming but mostly fanciful stories (Vicary's 'subliminal advertising' was a godsend). The researchers he interviewed were put in an impossible situation – if they talked openly and even naively, as many did, they gave Packard plenty of material that could easily be made to sound deeply sinister; if, on the other hand, they weren't so open, or backtracked, they appeared defensive and looked as if they had something to hide. But at the heart of Packard's attack is a strand of truth which advertising folk themselves have often found uncomfortable – the fact that much advertising does indeed influence people's behaviour in ways other than conscious, rational argument. If we accept this as a fact –and today it is increasingly hard not to - we may have to allow a debate about the ethical implications of it, and where if anywhere society should set limits to it. But on the whole, advertising theorists have much preferred not to accept it as a fact.

So was Packard the murderer? He looks like the obvious

culprit, and maybe in a sense he was. But my guess is that while Packard created the context, the actual death blow didn't come until a few years later. And it was to be dealt by someone inside the ad industry.

In Chapter Four I introduced Rosser Reeves, the head of the Ted Bates agency, and his 1961 book *Reality in Advertising*. I argued that Reeves's central concept of the Unique Selling Proposition did a great deal to re-establish the idea of message transmission as the central model of advertising, a position it has arguably maintained to this day. To understand Reeves's position properly, however, we need to look at it in the context of its time, and especially of the runaway popular success of *The Hidden Persuaders*.

Reeves's title always struck me as a little odd, until I realised that it must be, surely, a deliberate response to Pierre Martineau's book, *Motivation in Advertising*. Martineau had argued for the importance of emotion, non-verbal communication, so-called 'depth' psychology – all the ways in which advertising influences its audiences other than through conscious, rational persuasion. This was the same material which Packard would present in the same year, but with his own spin on it, in which anything other than honest, factual salesmanship was equated with evil manipulation. Reeves's book, I believe, served two agendas. First, it was an unashamed puff for Reeves's agency, defending his 'salesmanship' model against the fashionable new theories of motivation research. But it was also a deliberate attempt by Reeves to distance not only his own agency, but the industry as a whole, from the slanders put upon it by Packard. Hence the title, whose point must surely have been clear to those in the business.

Reeves's position becomes most explicit in the chapter which he calls 'The Freudian Hoax', in which he pooh-poohs the claims of depth psychology. There are, he writes,

...no hidden persuaders.
Advertising works openly, in the bare and pitiless sunlight.(p.70)

And maybe there was a third agenda too: I think at a deeper level, Reeves may have been defending the creative territory of the admen against the presumptions of the researchers, and in doing this he spoke on behalf of many – including creative gurus like Bernbach. We might imagine today that Bernbach and Reeves were diametrically opposed, and in some ways they were, but they also had a lot in common, as I shall explore in a moment. And I'm hypothesising now that both of them would have found great satisfaction in getting those upstart motivation researchers off their creative patch.

Whoever struck the death blow, use of the expression 'motivation research' rapidly declined after about 1960. Analysis, using Google Books Ngram Viewer, shows that the phrase first appeared in 1951, peaked in 1959, and fell sharply from 1961 (the year of Reeves's book), so that its use in 1964 was already less than 40% of the peak; it has continued to decline ever since. ('Hidden persuaders', interestingly, peaks in 1963, six years after Packard's book was first published, then follows a similar decline. Make of this what you will: Appendix 2.)

And as motivation research was rapidly airbrushed from history, something important shifted in the discourse that was professionally permissible about advertising. This shift was simple: any mention of 'the unconscious' was now off limits. This left the 'scientific' approach to advertising only one route to explore, and fortunately this was a route that easily lent itself to measurement – the route of message transmission and attitude change. Communication had to be seen to be conscious and therefore, effectively, rational and capable of being put into words. The non-rational aspects of choice were allowed in only through the established sociological construct of 'attitudes', which had been explored in the thirties by people like Allport, Guttman, and Likert in order to understand issues such as racial prejudice (Krech et al, 1962). But the ways in which attitudes were understood and measured were themselves heavily dependent on verbal statements, and when these techniques had been considerably further simplified and bastardised for use in market research they tended towards the norm of scales based on functional attributes, such as 'X gets my wash really clean', or at most, conscious expressions of perceptions that should more usefully have been thought of as unconscious and measured by projective techniques, such as 'a brand for young people'. These basic assumptions set the framework for market and advertising research that has persisted, with only marginal dissent, until the present.

Chapter Seven:

There's One Little Rub

Bill Bernbach and the 'Benign Conspiracy'

any people in advertising must have remained convinced that these measures were missing out something important, but found it increasingly hard to argue for what it was. No longer able to use the forbidden language of unconscious processes, the full authority of both 'science' and 'measurement' forced them to acknowledge a model of fact-based persuasion. Unable to argue their case *within* the scientific discourse, many took refuge in a fundamentally different set of values – the discourse of art. It is therefore no coincidence that the sixties saw not only the growing dominance of the post-Reeves and *DAGMAR* rational, persuasion-based models, but also became the heyday of what has been called the creative revolution – the flourishing of advertising professionals who had enough confidence and charisma openly to belittle the power of research and to assert that intuition and judgement were more important.

In this way, the schizophrenia of modern advertising was forged. On one side, the apparent might of Science, or to be more accurate, something that looked like Science, offered measurement, predictability and control to the responsible business leader. On the other side, there remained a profound but largely inarticulate recognition that this conscious, rational model was missing out the most important things about how advertising really worked. But as any 'science of the unconscious' was now unmentionable, this view could only base its alternative authority on the inspired and frequently temperamental figure of the Artist.

Despite important differences, the creative revolution led by Bernbach continued to share some of its most fundamental assumptions with Rosser Reeves. In Bernbach's own writings he is careful to avoid any language that suggests the subconscious, and he eschews words such as *symbolism,* or even *associations.* On the contrary, he frequently asserts that 'the magic is in the product' and that all advertising starts with a clear and single minded 'proposition'. Even when he argues that '*how* you say it' is as important as 'what you say', his choice of language privileges the verbal. When he wants to go beyond the realm of logic, it is not into the dangerous territory of 'the non-rational', but the aspirational realm of 'artistry'.

> Make sure your *proposition* is right, then let your people *say* it incisively, artfully, unforgettably. (1980, *emphasis added*)

> The purpose of advertising, I repeat, is to sell. (1971)

And rather than attack Rosser Reeves (with whom I think he was always on good terms*), Bernbach typically accepted his position, and then patronisingly went beyond it:

> A unique selling proposition is no longer enough. Without a unique selling talent, it may die.(1980)

This discourse served Bernbach and his successors well for two reasons. Firstly, it created common ground with clients whose fundamental assumption was a sales-based model of advertising – sure, it says, we're salesmen too, but we're more effective because we're salesmen with artistry. And artistry is important because it attracts *attention* and it makes the message more *memorable*: points one and five of Starch's 1923 hierarchical model.

> For a speaker on advertising not to express the importance of creativity in *getting attention to an ad* and *making the product advantage memorable* is almost criminal negligence. (1980, *emphasis added*)

Second, it completely dissociates the agency's creative wizardry from the rival authority of researchers, psychologists, sociologists, and other boffins. 'Persuasion isn't a science, it's an art': and Bernbach continually stresses how the crucial factor in successful advertising is something that can't be defined, analysed, or reduced to logic.

Although Bernbach never wrote a book, his various articles

---

* David Ogilvy recalls having Bill Bernbach and Rosser Reeves as his lunch guests, towards the end of Bernbach's life: 'Bill lectured us both as if we were trainees at his agency'.

and speeches have been so much quoted that I think he is a major influence on modern discourses about advertising, especially in creative departments. He has set up an interesting and paradoxical version of reality which most agencies still live with. On the one hand, advertising is still seen as a matter of logic, facts, and salesmanship: the product, the proposition, the single-minded thing you say. This is fair game for discussion, logic, analysis. But what then makes this work is something beyond discussion, because it's to do with taste, artistry, magic… all those words that exist to close down discussion, rather than invite it. It's a bit like the dualism that entered into philosophy about the time of Descartes. Science could deal with physical things, but when you got into talking about the mind this was a bit too close to the spiritual; it was understood that science didn't trespass on the authority of the church, and that division was important because in the state of debate that then existed about religion, it was better not to go there if you didn't want to lose your job or your head. Bernbach, I think rather brilliantly, set up a similar boundary around creative departments, which has served them well ever since.

But has it served advertising well? Up to a point, I think it did. It created what my friend Robert Heath once called the 'benign conspiracy'. Clients and suits and planners could bother their heads arguing about target audiences and propositions and so forth. Once this was agreed, their main task had been done, everyone could congratulate themselves on being clever and businesslike and responsible, and the brief then went to the creative department. And they – on a good day – would do something utterly unexpected and intuitive that might or might not bear any relationship to the brief, and with a following wind it would run and achieve brilliant results for reasons that had nothing to do with the proposition or the functional benefit. I think that fits a lot of the best advertising that was done throughout the seventies and eighties, and maybe still happens occasionally today.

But it served the advertising less well when clients started taking their own logic too literally, especially through the mechanism of research. If an ad was really to be dismembered to fit the procrustean bed of the creative brief, it was almost certain to end up dead on arrival. That's why, although part of me would like to go back to those innocent days of the benign conspiracy, I'm not sure we can. I think we may have to learn to be more honest with ourselves, about what we know and don't know, where we can make use of analytical thought and where we shouldn't, and take on board some fairly incontrovertible facts about how people make decisions and how communications work.

There's one more highly influential writer and adman who I have to include in this narrative, because he perhaps more than any other tried to have it both ways – arguing both for the power of the 'brand image' and the importance of creativity, and for the centrality of rational persuasion and the value of research-based rules. I'm not sure that he ever found a satisfactory way of reconciling these two views, either in theory or in practice, and over time it appears that the rational persuasion model became more predominant. David Ogilvy matters in our story because he published not one but two best-selling books on advertising (even if the second one is not shy of recycling material from the first); and it is a safe bet that if any client or agency employee has read one book on advertising, it will be *Confessions of an Advertising Man* or (more likely) *Ogilvy on Advertising*.

Ogilvy's agency came to fame in the fifties through a series of campaigns for small, upscale clients – Hathaway, Schweppes, Rolls-Royce. The ads are still well-known and celebrated in advertising circles. For Hathaway, a small US shirt manufacturer, Ogilvy chose as model a man with an air of mystery and class, one Baron Wrangel. On the day of the shoot Ogilvy appeared with a box of eye-patches and suggested Wrangel should wear one. 'The Man in the Hathaway Shirt' became hugely successful, with his signature (never explained) eye-patch – so much so that future ads in the series dispensed with copy, and eventually even the brand name. For Schweppes Ogilvy did something similar, featuring the eccentrically bearded Commander Whitehead, Schweppes's US sales manager, in every ad. Whatever these campaigns were doing (both, very successfully), it had nothing to with claims or propositions. Yet Ogilvy – who was Rosser Reeves's brother in law – argued strongly in his books for Claude Hopkins's claim-based theories, for factual copy and for headlines based on rules (Ogilvy had started as a researcher for Gallup).

Is it just coincidence that, after about 1960, the output of Ogilvy's agency became less and less like the early, whimsical, visual campaigns that made his name – and more and more claim-based, even if not usually quite as crudely as those of his brother-in-law? Perhaps it was part of the agency's growth trajectory – or perhaps this too was Ogilvy's own way of distancing himself from the accusations of *The Hidden Persuaders*. Vance Packard had, after all, featured the Man in the Hathaway Shirt in his book, as an example of a 'nonrational symbol' – and without actually saying anything about why this might be wrong, heavily insinuated, in his characteristic way, that it was somehow deeply sinister.

Looking back, the fifties in the US and the UK was a decade of booming growth for advertising – a time of unprecedented prosperity in the US, and the first real decade of commercial television, a medium which proved to be more potent than any before it. This growth also fuelled an intellectual ferment and experimentation which I don't think we've ever seen since in advertising, though a lot of people have looked for it (I think, in vain) in the rise of the internet. New and competing theories of the advertising process co-existed in an exciting plurality of views: new perspectives on human behaviour influenced creative theories of artistry and intuition, and gave us campaigns like the Marlboro Man and Tony the Tiger. Martin Mayer's book is still the most fascinating for me about advertising because it precisely describes the height of this ferment – a spectrum of larger than life agency bosses, creatives, researchers, and media folk, representing a spectrum of different approaches, and all successfully, from Rosser Reeves to Dichter, from Bernbach to Politz.

This plurality of views, this energetic bubbling up of ideas, did not - perhaps could not - last. Somewhere around 1960 it began to cool down and coalesce into a set pattern that is still recognisable today. I have argued that Vance Packard and Rosser Reeves played an important role in the way this pattern emerged, though I think it also fair to say that they both represented larger forces that would probably have prevailed anyway – the need for clients, agencies, and the public alike to cling to their self-image as 'rational', autonomous decision makers. When 'Motivation Research' suddenly disappeared as a concept, along with it seemed to go any language for talking about subconscious processing, emotional decision making, psychological needs, or symbolism. This made a lasting impact on our shared models of advertising. But no-one, it seems, was sorry to see 'MR' go. For advertisers and agencies alike, it had become an embarrassing stick for critics of advertising to beat them with. For research companies, it left them with plenty of scope for simpler forms of survey research based on DAGMAR thinking, that were both easier for clients to understand and more profitable at scale. For creative directors, it removed a threat to their authority as the only people who added the intangible magic.

The pattern that now emerged was what I have described as the dualistic view, or at its best, the benign conspiracy. On the one hand, accepted theories of advertising reverted to a version of the salesmanship model which I described in Part One, including all its internal contradictions. Advertising was planned and researched on the basis that it first attracted attention, then transmitted a message or proposition, which had to be understood, believed, and remembered. At the same time, it was more or less accepted – more in creative departments, rather less among some clients, with the account managers keeping the peace – that something intangible called 'creativity', which defied analysis or debate, was an essential ingredient. But when challenged to justify why it was so important, the logic reverted again to the message transmission model – you needed creativity in order to attract attention to the ad, and to increase the memorability of the message. Other possibilities were hardly considered.

At its best, this could be a negotiated truce, a division of powers that allowed effective work to emerge, the benign conspiracy. Although it would give rise to endless border disputes over the next sixty years, at a larger level the formula kept the peace. Even today, I have a strong sense that challenges to this model feel to many people like a threat to their own position within a delicately poised balance of powers. Theories of how advertising works are not innocent. They are intimately bound up with power relations, and also with deeper world views which legitimate power relations. So theories of how advertising works, however implicit, have an impact on power relations within the agency, and between the agency and the client. A theory which is based on intuition and taste will privilege the creative department; a theory which is based on psychological insight may give power to the planning department; a theory based on measurement of message recall gives authority to the researchers and thus to the client. Most client organisations have a requirement that decisions should be justifiable, in a way that is verbal, logical, quantifiable, and preferably simple. A proposition based model of advertising serves this requirement well, even if it serves little else. The client organisation may also require that its world view takes precedence over the agency's world view, thus ensuring that a model that fits that world view will prevail. (If you never understood Foucault's theory of the relationship between knowledge and power before, this is a good example of it.)

Yet to anyone who takes the trouble to look hard at actual campaigns and consider how they achieve their results, this dualistic approach has always been deeply unsatisfactory. In the final chapter of this section I want to consider another movement that attempted to challenge this new consensus, one that allows me to bring myself into the story a little – the British account planning movement.

Chapter Eight:

Camay is a Bit Catty

Stephen King and the Account Planning Movement

J ust after writing the previous chapter, I found a 1971 paper by Mary Tuck, a copywriter at J. Walter Thompson (JWT) in London during the fifties who later became a market researcher and academic. There are moments in writing this sort of stuff when, I confess, I wonder how much I'm just making up with the wisdom of hindsight - so it was rather exciting to find this paragraph, a rather precise contemporary endorsement of the 'benign conspiracy' I outlined just now:

> Of course, in a sense the 'creative' approach and the 'content' approach can work very well together. The marketing man, researcher or planner comes up with the right 'message' through carrying out vast blockbuster studies of 'attitudes'. The creative man is asked to produce an advertisement which expresses this message in a striking and attractive way. This is perhaps the most widely spread way of creating advertisements right now in London. (p.55)

Then Mary Tuck continues as follows:

> But there has always been a strong school of
> dissent. Stephen King pointed out in 1965 that to
> separate style and content is an artificial exercise.
> A consumer responds to a message as a totality.

This is a very good introduction to what account planning
was really all about. On the face of it, it was about agency
reorganisation. But its origins lay in deep dissatisfaction
with the theories of advertising then in use. The
dissatisfaction was itself founded in experience, empirical
research, and influenced by alternative perspectives from
the social sciences (Feldwick, 2007). Well before 1968, its
official birth, the genesis of account planning was taking
place in JWT London under Stephen King (Director of
Research), John Treasure (Chairman), Timothy Joyce and
others; while at Pritchard Wood and Partners (PWP),
Stanley Pollitt, an account director newly in charge of the
agency research department, was becoming increasingly
frustrated by the irrelevance of most of the data on offer.
(The entire management of PWP would leave in 1968 to
found Boase Massimi Pollitt (BMP), where account
planning would be 'built in' to the agency from the outset.)

As Mary Tuck observed, the pioneers of planning were
sceptical of the ideas that advertising worked by rational
persuasion, or the transmission of predominantly verbal
messages. An influential paper in 1967 by Timothy Joyce,
of JWT's research partner company, BMRB, expressed
some of their key doubts. The idea that advertising
converts people from Brand A to Brand B was misleading –

advertising is largely a matter of 'exploiting and reinforcing the already favourable attitudes of people who may be users at least in a broad sense'. Attitudes may influence purchasing, but purchasing also influences attitudes. 'Consumers' decisions cannot be fitted to a model of rational choice...', wrote Joyce: 'The "rational argument" model of advertising is therefore generally inappropriate' (p.37). In general, the picture beginning to emerge from JWT/BMRB was very different from the 'conversion' model that had been implicit in most advertising thinking ever since Claude Hopkins had applied his experiences as a travelling preacher and snake oil salesman to advertising. The role of advertising was to reinforce and nurture preferences for a particular brand, and these preferences were largely based on emotional and non-verbal cues.

Stephen King expressed these arguments over many years in numerous articles, most of which are now available in the excellent volume edited by Judie Lannon and Merry Baskin. In papers such as 'What is a Brand?' (1970), he developed the concept of branding as central to advertising and marketing, using the idea of the *gestalt* or whole to emphasise that this was how consumers experienced brands – as a totality, not as a collection of elements. You may remember that Ernest Dichter claimed to have invented the term 'brand image' as a translation of the word *gestalt*. It's interesting to me, however, that King and his contemporaries make little or no reference in their writings to Dichter, Martineau, or 'motivation research', although they must have been familiar with them. They were in some ways following in their tracks, but I'm guessing that they didn't want to contaminate their arguments with the toxic legacy of *The Hidden Persuaders*. So, finding alternative conceptual frameworks in disciplines such as anthropology, they succeeded in creating their own rather British, understated version of brand theory which avoided any mention of the 'subconscious', or, heaven forbid, Freud. King's writings throughout adopt a splendidly unpretentious, everyday language for explaining what could have seemed complex or academic ideas; he did, after all, want to sell this as a basis for practice to some pretty hard nosed clients.

> People choose their brands as they choose their friends. You choose friends not usually because of specific skills or physical attributes (though of course these come into it) but simply because you like them as people. It is the total person you choose, not a compendium of virtues and vices. (Lannon and Baskin, p.32)

Qualitative research played a central part in this new way of understanding brand-consumer relationships, but again King and his contemporaries were careful to avoid jargon of 'depth' or 'psychology' – it was just presented as an everyday matter:

> Once you have heard people describing Lifebuoy as rather abrupt, Tide as gruff and ex-army, Camay as a bit catty, will you be content to rely solely on the sort of research that gets people to put crosses on a seven point scale running from 'kind to the hands' to 'not so kind to the hands'? (p.40)

Another of Stephen King's significant contributions to advertising thinking was a recognition that different ads, after all, might actually be trying to do different things. The classic mail order ad invites an immediate response in the form of a sale, while at the opposite extreme a typical 'brand image' ad aims to reinforce existing attitudes in order to defend brand share. In between these two points, King devised his 'scale of immediacy', in which different advertisements were either closer to or further away from (in time and/or space) the action which, in every case, represented the only logical goal of advertising (pp.124-136).

This was not an entirely new thought, though it is remarkable enough that as late as 1975 (when it was presented at a Market Research Society Conference), it could still be seen as something of a breakthrough. The idea that different ads work in different ways because they are setting out to do different things was acknowledged in Starch's *Principles of Advertising* in 1923, and, to give Russell Colley his due, is also inherent in the thinking of *DAGMAR*. If Stephen King was indebted to any previous thinker, however, it was to a predecessor of his at J. Walter Thompson – James Webb Young.

Young was born in 1886 in Cincinnati, and joined JWT in 1912 as a copywriter. In a long and distinguished career he fulfilled many important roles, besides writing some very famous campaigns – he helped to sort out the US advertising commission system, he set up several of the European offices of JWT, and was founder and Chairman of the US Advertising Council. In 1928 (aged 42) he decided to 'retire' to a ranch in New Mexico where he sold his own apples by mail order, and in the following decade also served as a professor at the University of Chicago business school, though he was later persuaded to return to JWT as a consultant and director.

In 1963 – in his late seventies, and still working for JWT – James Webb Young published a short book, *How to Become an Advertising Man*, based on the lectures he had given at Chicago in the 1930s. Young begins by recommending the now familiar concepts of proposition, attention, and message. His more original contribution to advertising thought comes in the later chapters, in which he proposes five ways in which advertising works: these are

- familiarising
- reminding
- spreading news
- overcoming inertias
- adding a value not in the product.

While not presented as a continuum, these can be mapped very loosely on to King's scale – overcoming inertia as the trigger to action in direct response, adding value as brand development, etc. (The last, 'adding a value not in the product', was especially important to King and his colleagues as a succinct - and less contentious - way to explain why people preferred certain brands and would pay more for them; the JWT planners were among the first to show that users' experience of a product was significantly different when it was branded. Thus, advertising helped create a real (subjective) value, from which brand buyers benefited.)

It is hard to argue with either Young's or King's typology, and both contrast dramatically with the implied assumption of Reeves or Hopkins that all ads are fundamentally the same. Both can be used in a practical way to help answer the question which King (and most later account planners) regarded as essential – what is the role for advertising in each situation? They are, if you like, useful heuristics or 'rules of thumb' for planning purposes; they are just not neat, watertight, or universally obvious ways of dividing up reality (as evidenced by the fact that they aren't identical with each other). King admits right at the outset:

> In real life, it is clear enough that many advertisements work at several points on the scale. (Lannon and Baskin,p.135)

And Young had already acknowledged that:

> ...whereas some advertising may soundly be devoted to one of these uses alone; and in nearly all advertising one of them will be primary; most advertising will involve two or more of these uses. (Young, p.50)

Nevertheless, this way of thinking marks a major advance on the conventional rhetoric of advertising from Hopkins to Bernbach which defines all outcomes indiscriminately as 'sales'.

I never worked at JWT, and although there were many similarities between the two original planning agencies, there were also differences. So it seems appropriate now to bring myself into the story a bit, and offer you some reflections on what we were doing – and what we thought we were doing – at BMP in the seventies and eighties.

Compared with JWT, then the biggest agency in London, BMP was a tiny creative hot shop. JWT planners had years of research and often media planning experience; BMP planners tended to be straight out of university, and, although many of us had first class degrees, the agency was in many ways deeply unintellectual. We did not theorise in the way JWT did about 'how advertising worked'. We just assumed that we knew, that the answer was obvious, and that most other people had got it badly wrong. If anything, I think we were discouraged from reading about earlier theories of advertising in case we became contaminated by them ourselves. For many years, I think this attitude of blinkered arrogance served us rather well. In the longer run, I think it may have left the agency vulnerable, but that is harder to prove.

We had a high ratio of planners to accounts, so that planners could typically immerse themselves in all aspects of the process from initial strategy through to campaign evaluation. Planners were expected to be numerate (I got in through a loophole because I didn't have A-Level maths, but luckily discovered I was numerate enough after all). We paid a lot of attention to market data and survey data, which in those days were oddly more accessible than they are now, but we paid equal or more attention to qualitative research, which we almost always conducted ourselves. Central to our way of working was using qualitative research groups to explore reactions to test commercials in 'animatic' form. (It was later said that while JWT planners were 'grand strategists', BMP planners were 'ad tweakers': there is some truth in this, though the choice of language is unfairly loaded. I still think getting the ads right is what's most important.)

'How ads work' was a question which we therefore confronted on a case by case basis, without too many preconceptions, rather than on a level of abstract and general theorising. This open-minded approach was reflected, during the first several years I was there, in the fact that we had no creative briefing form whatsoever: you wrote whatever needed to be said, and preferably made it the basis for a conversation rather than simply an order passed to the kitchen. I still think this is a very good way to work, though it was always a risky strategy – done well it's brilliant, done badly it's garbage. (But that's true of creative briefing forms too.) What kept us grounded throughout these improvisatory processes was the amount of qualitative research the planners did, and a power structure that ensured that this was always taken seriously within the agency. Perhaps most importantly our creative director, John Webster, enjoyed working with account planners, and his creativity usually seemed to be stimulated by the feedback from our qualitative research. I later realised that John was unusual, perhaps even unique, in this regard.

We were also fortunate in that we found clients who were prepared to work with us in this way, not because they were naïve (though some were), but generally because they were relatively unencumbered with corporate advertising manuals that mandated briefing forms and research protocols.

But insofar as we did have a general theory of advertising, it went something like this, as explained to me by Martin Boase at some point during my first few weeks at the agency. He said – I paraphrase his words – 'We believe that if you're going to invite yourself into someone's living room for thirty seconds, you have a duty not to bore them or insult them by shouting at them. On the other hand, if you can make them smile, or show them something interesting or enjoyable – if you're a charming guest – then they may like you a bit better, and then they may be a little more likely to buy your product.' I remember at the time this struck me as rather whimsical: but as I will explain later (Chapter 13) it now seems to me one of the most perceptive things I've ever heard about advertising.

You could also interpret our working methods as another version of the benign conspiracy. The planners offered logical thinking to reassure the clients; the creatives largely did as they pleased; the planners post-rationalised. This sounds a little cynical, but it wasn't: what held it all together successfully was the continual grounding in qualitative research, before, during and after the campaign, and a genuine commitment which I have never seen surpassed to an agency goal of 'getting the advertising right at all costs' – as Stanley Pollitt said, 'Getting it right being more important than maximising agency profits, more important than keeping clients happy, or building an agency shop window for distinctive-looking advertising.' (Lannon and Baskin, p.21).

I have to admit that as time passed, it became more and more difficult to maintain this way of working. Clients became more insistent on us doing things their way.

They argued more often against us doing qualitative research (sometimes in the very unfair belief that we would favour our own work – that was never true). They insisted more on using quant pre-test methodologies which we believed had been discredited many years ago but then returned with a vengeance. We merged with DDB, whose London office had inherited its founder's wholesale scepticism about research, and gradually things changed. Both clients and creative-led agency justified their position with reference to the incontrovertible rightness of the proposition-led model, and I think it must have been around this time that I began to see the relevance of understanding the historical and contingent roots of these accepted models.

The British account planning movement can claim one other important development in advertising thinking. This was the launch in 1980 of the Institute of Practitioners in Advertising (IPA) Advertising Effectiveness Awards; these were the brainchild of Simon Broadbent, a fiercely intelligent statistician and media planner who worked for Leo Burnett in London. Broadbent's mission, in which he was strongly supported by Stephen King and other leading account planners, was to create a library of case studies that would rigorously demonstrate the *business* results of advertising. Since the time of DAGMAR, or in practice long before, it had been orthodoxy that sales effects were not measurable, and therefore advertising outcomes could only be based on intermediate measures such as awareness or brand attitudes. Yet the relevance of such measures depended on certain assumptions about how advertising works being valid, and it was just these assumptions which were now being called into question. The IPA Awards challenged the industry to find better ways to link advertising to hard business outcomes; as a result, the ad industry's attitude to measuring effectiveness has been largely transformed, with more extensive use of econometric analysis and better understanding of long-term effects as two specific developments. Increasingly, the evidence from this ongoing project shows that what really works in a business sense need not conform to any single theory, and certainly need not contain a proposition or a reason why (Binet and Field).

*

In Part Two I have tried to describe some influential counter-currents in advertising thought which have tried to justify, in one way or another, a very different point of view from the 'rational persuasion' orthodoxy considered in Part One. There are strong arguments that advertising is not principally a matter of rational persuasion, that it works in ways of which the audience is often not entirely aware, that it reinforces or nudges or charms or seduces more effectively than it argues or educates or converts. Over time, however, the orthodoxy of rational persuasion keeps bouncing back, regardless of its weaknesses, and still maintains its dominance today – perhaps more to the detriment of effective advertising than ever.

But perhaps this polarity between two opposed schools of thought – a polarity to which I have made my own contributions over the years – is itself a mistake? Perhaps neither is as simplistically 'right' or 'wrong' as its adherents or supporters think it is. Perhaps there are even other ways of thinking about advertising that are different again from these two dominant streams of thinking, and perhaps all of them have their own validity and something useful to offer. In Part Three I explore both these possibilities.

Part Three:

Six Aspects of
the Elephant

So oft in theologic wars
The disputants, I ween,
Rail on in utter ignorance
Of what each other mean
And prate about an Elephant
Not one of them has seen!

John G. Saxe (1816-1887), 'The Blind Men
and the Elephant' (in Cady, p.452)

Chapter Nine:

The Whole Elephant

Six Ways of Thinking about Advertising

So far we have explored two principal 'family trees' of advertising thinking – what I have called the 'Salesmanship' tradition, based on rational, conscious persuasion and the transmission of messages, and its counterpart, 'Seduction', which emphasises the power of non-verbal, unconscious communication and the importance of emotions in decision making. We haven't yet finished with either of these, because I want to reflect further on the ways in which each can be useful, and also on their limitations, and I shall do that in the next two chapters.

But while these two traditions have some claim to have been the dominant ones in the history of advertising thought, as expressed in the discourse of its practitioners, they by no means exhaust all the possibilities of how we might choose to think about advertising. So in this third section of the book I also want to introduce some alternatives. That I have devoted less space to them doesn't mean that I think they are necessarily less useful or important; though it may reflect the fact that they have tended to be on the fringes of orthodox advertising discourse rather than at its centre. But maybe if we ad people are as good at 'thinking outside the box' as we say we are, we could benefit from taking them more seriously.

I was fond of a poem in my childhood which for many years has seemed appropriate to understanding how advertising works. Perhaps you know it, and perhaps you will excuse any possible hints of political incorrectness in the set-up, considering that it was written well over a hundred years ago. It is called 'The Blind Men and the Elephant', and it begins like this:

> It was six men of Indostan
> To learning much inclined
> Who went to see the elephant
> (Though all of them were blind),
> That each by observation
> Might satisfy his mind.

Each of the men approaches the elephant and encountering a different part of the beast, describes it in a way that has no conceivable connection with each of the others: for example one walks into its side and declares the elephant 'very like a wall', one finds the trunk and announces it is 'very like a snake', one takes the tusk and concludes that the elephant is very like a spear, and so on: the leg is like a tree, the tail like a rope, the ear like a leaf.

> And so these men of Indostan
> Disputed loud and long,
> Each in his own opinion
> Exceeding stiff and strong,

Though each was partly in the right
And all were in the wrong!

It's in that spirit that I suggest we might consider this question of advertising. Part of our problem has always been that we want it to be easy, we want it to be simple; we want something that can be written in the corporate manual and sent around the world, that people can be trained to do in a half day session, that can be measured using a few standard questions, that will enable us to create a single creative briefing form. But advertising ain't like that. The mysterious and perhaps infinite ways in which one published utterance in any medium may influence one person's choice behaviour can involve everything we know, and more importantly, everything we don't know and perhaps will never know, about how we make choices, how we perceive things, what motivates us, how we influence each other, how memory works, how we construct reality, OK, life the universe and everything.

At this point some practical people will put their hands up – as Gordon Brown (of Millward Brown) did to me once - and say well this is all no good, if it's impossibly complicated where are we to start? But I'm not advocating this position except as an acknowledgement that we will never find a comprehensive, objective watertight set of answers, however much we might like them. However, based on many decades of practical experience, and our current understanding of the human sciences, we can put together a set of possible tools, or heuristics if you like, for thinking about it in a practical sense.

In memory of The Blind Men and the Elephant, I've therefore added four more traditions – four more ways of seeing – to the original two, giving us a total of six. You could also imagine these as the six sides of a cube, maybe even a Rubik's cube where all the different facets of the same reality are interconnected. Apart from these conceits, of course, the number six is quite arbitrary, and you might well make a case for adding more (or maybe rolling two of these together). But six is a good number to remember, and it seemed adequate to covering what I wanted to say here, so I'm sticking with it for now.

So what, you may be curious to know, are the other four facets of the cube? I'll give you just their chapter headings for the moment, and as I come to each in turn I'll do my best to explain the thinking behind them. I shall name all six as follows:

1. Advertising as Salesmanship
2. Advertising as Seduction
3. Advertising as Salience
4. Advertising as Social Connection
5. Advertising as Spin
6. Advertising as Showbiz

I have chosen each of these because they both represent a theoretical position – sometimes quite a sophisticated one – but more importantly because each represents some kind of actual practice. Some may feel more familiar than others. I urge you to persevere with the ones that feel less familiar, because after all, we should all be interested in new ways of thinking about advertising, should we not – just as

Albert Lasker was when John Kennedy sent his note in all those years ago?

And I want to repeat again that these are not to be understood as rival or mutually exclusive theories – they are all intended as different ways of thinking about the same thing, all of which may have their uses, and each of which alone has its limitations. My model for this way of proceeding, by the way, is a marvellous book by Gareth Morgan called *Images of Organization* which does a similar thing – under nine chapter headings – for ways of thinking about organisations – as a machine, as an organism, etc. Nor is it just as simple as saying that some ads fit one model, some fit another. While you may well find that some models make better sense of individual ads than others, most ads, and maybe even all ads, can be interpreted through the lens of more than one way of thinking, and quite possibly of all six. Every ad, if you like, is potentially at least an entire elephant.

Chapter Ten:

Your Flies are Undone!

The Pros and Cons of Propositions

A s we have seen, 'advertising as rational persuasion' is not a single coherent theory. It includes Hopkins's long copy ads and 'reason why' as well as Reeves's single USP - it can lead to an emphasis on attention or to message recall – indeed it can result in some flatly contradictory principles, which is part of its weakness. As a 'way of thinking about advertising', however, it is relatively coherent and based on some common principles: that advertising is a matter of rational persuasion, that it works consciously and must therefore begin by attracting conscious attention, that persuasion depends on transmitting messages and that these messages must be understood and believed, that the message should be based around a proposition or benefit, and that the proposition or benefit must where appropriate be lodged in long term memory.

Stated like that, I can imagine many readers still thinking – and what's so wrong about all that? Isn't it, after all, exactly what we've always been taught? My point is not that this way of thinking is inherently 'wrong'. It would be very odd to argue that, because so many successful advertising practitioners have used it in one way or another. In some ways it is both well-founded and useful, and I will go on to review exactly what those ways might be. It is a way of thinking that we can continue to make good use of in the future. However I will begin by arguing that it also misses out a great deal, and that when it is applied too literally – as it frequently is - it becomes a constraint rather than an enabler.

I remember many years ago giving a lecture at a seminar in Istanbul, at which there was present a formidable lady, the doyenne of the Turkish advertising research industry. As part of my talk I presented some case histories from the IPA awards, including a campaign for a brand of cough sweet called Strepsils. When it came to question time, this woman put her hand up. Looking fiercely at me, she said with total conviction 'It is not possible that this campaign was successful. The commercial contains no consumer benefit.' It mattered not to her that I had shown robust, IPA approved evidence for sales effects. It did not fit her theory and therefore could not work.

This demonstrates the danger of being trapped in any single theory, to be sure, but in my experience it most commonly applies to the rational persuasion type of theory – partly because it is the most dominant, and partly because it is the simplest to understand and judge ads by. And thereby lies part of its continuing appeal. But the principal weakness of this model is that those who become attached to it – and many unsurprisingly are, as it is still taught as dogma in many circles – refuse to believe in other possibilities for advertising to influence behaviour, despite the fact that the scientific evidence for those other possibilities is probably far stronger than the evidence for the power of rational persuasion. In fact, a second fundamental weakness of the persuasion based models is that, as Stephen King pointed out many years ago, the axioms behind them are based on mere assertion, never on scientific evidence. Reeves offered no evidence for his claim that 'people remember only one thing from an advertisement', and I for one don't believe it's true. Russell Colley, the management consultant who wrote DAGMAR, introduced it by claiming its principles were 'applied common sense'. Yet common sense is the opposite of science. Common sense tells us that the sun is smaller than the earth and moves around it, or that a heavier item will fall to the ground faster: as Lewis Wolpert has pointed out, science is only needed at all because common sense is so often wrong. The origins of the rational persuasion theories lie entirely with practitioners following their hunches, and expressing them forcefully and plausibly – Kennedy, Hopkins, Reeves, Colley, and even Bernbach. They may appear scientific to many because they lend themselves easily to measurement, but scientific is just what they are not.

The third weakness I will claim for this model is that it so obviously fails to fit even a brief observation of actual campaigns which we know to be successful, as was so eloquently pointed out in the passage I quoted previously from Martineau which concluded: '... so much more is going on than just a sales argument with the consumer' (p. 75). It is interesting to compare Reeves's espoused theory with the ads his own agency produced – look up, for example, the Bates commercials for the painkiller Anacin which you can find today on YouTube. Sure, they are intrusive, irritating, and full of information. But you can notice two other things. One is, there's *lots* of information – it's much closer to Hopkins's idea of 'the more you tell, the more you sell', than to Reeves's own notion of the 'Unique' Proposition. More importantly, notice the importance of non-verbal imagery. A headache is visualised as a hammer beating on a skull, with a painful noise, only relieved by the pill; and as in so many Bates ads, most of the information is delivered by a man in a white coat. Even then, they weren't allowed to say he was a doctor, but they didn't need to - there's good evidence from psychological experiments that a white coat alone is enough to create a powerful authority figure, whom nurses will obey even against their own better judgement. Far from Reeves's own advertising working 'in the bare and pitiless sunlight', as he claimed, it uses subconscious manipulation (if you want to call it that) quite as much as anyone else.

We can judge the relative importance of rational persuasion in advertising by looking at the many campaigns that have won IPA and other effectiveness awards, and judging how many of these depend primarily on rational persuasion rather than anything else for their effects. Les Binet and Peter Field have done this analysis for us in the case of the IPA, and the results are clear – campaigns based on 'fame' and 'emotion' are much more likely to be successful , and successful on a greater scale, than those that depend on rational appeals.

There are therefore significant weaknesses in this way of thinking, and they become extremely dangerous when the model is applied rigorously and unthinkingly, especially through the medium of research. In an earlier paper, Robert Heath and I published the story of a highly successful campaign that had failed badly in pretesting research because the questions asked – what information was it giving about the product, was there anything you found hard to understand, etc – were entirely inappropriate to an ad that was better understood as pure entertainment. No doubt you have your own examples of this.

Having acknowledged all that, let's consider what the positive merits of this model might be. I believe there are some, and the ad industry would do well to focus on them more.

First, let's recognise the power of information, and not least verbal information. We may have forgotten about this because so much of what actually appears in ads today is extremely uninteresting; it might almost be called non-information. I open the nearest newspaper and take the first bit of advertising copy I find: it goes like this –

The XXX Wireless Audio System has been designed with you in mind. Beautifully crafted to suit any living space, this is how music should be enjoyed. Play with no limits, having the freedom to control how you listen, the way you want, whatever your style.

It's not surprising people think 'copy is dead': if this is all it can do, it deserves to be put out of its misery at once. But I'm not talking – yet – about how the myriad possibilities of the English language are being ignored here; I'm just talking about information. I turn a couple of pages and light on a different ad.

More than four million children's lives have been devastated by Typhoon Haiyan. Many are in urgent need of food, clean water and shelter. Without your help, more children's lives could be lost.

UNICEF is on the ground in the Philippines right now – and our emergency supplies are getting through. £30 from you could help provide safe water kits for three vulnerable families.

It's not particularly original, not deathless prose, but it gives me some information that might well motivate me to act – I probably knew about the disaster, of course, but I want to know now what I can do to help and that UNICEF will be able to use my money, and that's what they tell me. As a result of this information, I may be more likely to act.

I once shared a platform with Jeremy Bullmore at a conference on the theme of 'Advertising: Information or Persuasion?'. I made a ponderous speech, and then Jeremy stood up and said, in a musing tone:

'When I go into a restaurant – and they bring me the bill – and it says at the bottom, Service not included – [longish pause] – is that information, or persuasion?'

(Never share a platform with Bullmore.)

There are plenty of simple verbal messages that may well evoke an emotional, and also a behavioural response:

- Your flies are undone!
- I'm leaving you for another man!
- The kitchen's on fire!

Few advertising headlines can compete with these, but 'Philippines Emergency – Four Million Children Affected' has a go. However, the fundamental difference between this ad and the one for the music centre is that the UNICEF is a direct response ad. The people who wrote it know that its only reason for being is in order to attract more money in direct response to it than it cost to produce and place the ad. They can be fairly sure that they'll achieve this, because they use certain rules and principles established over the past century, and they'll finesse it further by measuring exactly how well alternative versions perform. These principles will not be very different from the principles Claude Hopkins wrote about: think of your audience as prospects wanting information, and give it to them. There's still plenty of room for advertising that does this, not least on the internet, and it's most obviously appropriate when the ad is actually 'selling' – take a look at any product offered on eBay for an example of information based, effective copy.

But does information count so much in a non-direct response situation? Earlier generations of professionals from Hopkins to Ogilvy badly overstated their case by arguing that all advertising follows the same rules as direct response – that is, and always was, patent nonsense. But in reacting against it, I wonder whether the industry has woefully undervalued the potential power of a strong claim or of detailed information. What else might that audio centre have told me about in its expensive national press space, for example? Who designed it, why it's better, where it's made, who recommends it, who else has got one, why it looks like it does, what does it sound like, how easy is it to operate, why did they bother, etc. etc.? And if there are no remotely interesting answers to any of those questions, why should I buy it? There are times when everyone could usefully remember John Kennedy's lecture to Lasker about the 'Reason Why' and at least explore the possibilities it opens up. There's no reason why the only ads with any copy in should be direct response ads – yet today that's almost universally true.

Perhaps I can sum up my thoughts about propositions and 'reasons why' like this. The idea that there *might* be a proposition and that there *might* be a reason why in your ad is exciting. It opens up possibilities. The idea that there *has to be* a proposition or that there *has to be* a reason why in your ad is deadening. It closes down possibilities – and it may force you into talking nonsense.

And while we've been taught to think exclusively about the idea of the 'proposition', we've largely forgotten that we could often more usefully think in terms of the 'story'. Propositions and stories are very different and we respond to them very differently. It's easy to argue with a proposition; it's impossible to argue with a story. Stories are generally far better at getting and keeping our attention, involving us emotionally, and lodging material in our memory – this is why great teachers throughout history have often used them. Journalists instinctively search for the 'story' – there's no reason that we in advertising shouldn't do the same.

I mentioned in the previous chapter how, from 1928 onwards, James Webb Young spent a lot of his time at his ranch in New Mexico. Here he produced and sold, mostly by mail order, 'Old Jim Young's Mountain Grown Apples' – for which, of course, he wrote the ads himself. One year a severe hailstorm struck the orchard, giving the apples a brown and spotty surface, though they still tasted perfect. Thousands of dollars' worth of fruit risked either being sold cheaply as seconds, or being rejected by disappointed customers. For some days Young was at a loss what to do. Then he woke in the night with an idea. When each customer opened their box of apples that year, they found a card inside reading as follows:

> 'Note the hail marks which appear as minor skin blemishes on some of these apples. These are proof of their growth at a high mountain altitude, where the sudden chills from mountain hail storms which these apples receive while growing help firm their flesh and develop the fruit sugars which give them their fine flavour'.
> (Sumner, p.192)

No-one asked for their money back; indeed, many specially requested 'hail-marked apples' the following year.

Is this a proposition or a 'reason why'? Is it a brilliant strategy, or a brilliant execution?

Or is it just a good story – told in human language, as used by one human to influence the perceptions and behaviour of others? And is that something too many writers of advertising have forgotten about?

Chapter Eleven:

A Halo of Spotless Elegance

Walter Dill Scott and the Theory of Associations

J ust as the 'rational persuasion' school of advertising thought is not entirely the Evil Empire that many modern planners think it is, so 'seducing the subconscious' (in Robert Heath's memorable phrase) may not be the panacea for all problems either. There's much to be said in favour of this way of thinking about advertising, and I'll begin by enlarging on its strengths. But I will also notice that it too has its limitations.

The last twenty years have seen the idea of the subconscious (or unconscious) become much more scientifically respectable. Most of the ideas that the motivation researchers of the fifties were excited about now have a great deal more evidence to support them, even though their application to advertising practice is still largely limited to things people say at conferences and books planners keep ostentatiously on their desks. There is a broad acknowledgement that human decision making is, after all, strongly influenced or even dominated by subconscious needs, processes, and associations, that most techniques for influencing behaviour depend on these, and that this is much more securely supported by research and theory in the fields of psychology and neuroscience than it used to be.

The principal difference is that the language, and to some extent, the concepts, have shifted. The discourse is no longer about the dark, frightening Freudian unconscious, something we might feel ashamed of admitting to, but what Timothy Wilson calls the 'adaptive unconscious', a universal and inescapable part of everyday life and decision making. Antonio Damasio has explored in a series of books his rather complex but compelling hypotheses about how all decision making is intimately related to emotions and feelings, so that in a sense there is no such thing as a purely 'rational' decision. Dan Ariely, Richard Thaler and Cass Sunstein, Daniel Kahneman, and Barry Schwartz have all represented the findings of more than thirty years' experimental social psychology research under the successful brand called 'behavioural economics'. The implications of all this for advertising have been well explored by Robert Heath, Phil Barden, and others.

There are a number of related strands to this improved understanding of human choice which include implicit memory, implicit learning, low attention processing, the importance of affect or emotion in choice, the power of heuristics, choice architecture, and so on. I won't attempt here to summarise this fascinating and important field (principal works of the authors named above are listed in the Bibliography). But there's one particular theme I find especially useful and relatively easy to get my head around, and I think it's one we could make more practical use of in our work. This is the idea of associations, and it interestingly links together not just the work of Martineau and contemporary psychologists, but also theories that were around well before Hopkins published *Scientific Advertising*.

The idea of associations is indeed very old – philosophers wrote books about it in the eighteenth century, and you can find it even in Aristotle – today we just have more neurological and psychological evidence and theory to back it up. The idea, in lay terms, is that we are continually making mental connections between different perceptions and different experiences, and for the most part we are doing this unconsciously. (Damasio explains this through his concept of *engrams*, in which neurons firing simultaneously and repeatedly create lasting 'pathways' or connections in the brain.) Our perceptions and our responses to stimuli are continually being influenced by the patterns of associations we have already laid down. We see someone who dimly reminds us of a person who bullied us at school and instantly dislike them; we are more likely to trust someone in a smart suit; we feel better wearing certain clothes than others because of the meanings they have for us; we prefer our beer in a tall glass; and so on. We instantly and subconsciously make links between images and ideas, images and emotions, and the patterns of these are continually influencing the choices we make.

It seems to have been intuitively clear to a lot of people that this has much to do with advertising, and indeed all aspects of marketing – design, packaging, distribution, pricing, the context in which the brand is seen, etc. Advertising has tremendous power to create associations between a brand and images that evoke feelings of happiness, excitement, reassurance, coolness, confidence, and so on. Early advertisers such as William Lever or Pears' Soap intuitively understood this when they bought artistic paintings of cute children and animals to associate with their brands. And it was also one of the earliest scientific theories about how advertising works.

In 1903 – shortly before Kennedy met Lasker and talked about 'salesmanship in print' and the 'reason why' – Walter Dill Scott, a professor at Northwestern University near Chicago, first published his book *The Psychology of Advertising*. It is a fascinating read. It does not present a single, simple theory of advertising - it allows room for both logical argument and less conscious effects - but it does put great emphasis on the fact that advertising is frequently powerfully effective without being consciously recalled, and that it works by a process of subconscious association or as Scott also calls it, 'suggestion'.

> The actual effect of modern advertising is not so much to convince as to suggest...we think that we are performing a deliberate act when we purchase an advertised commodity, while in fact we may never have deliberated on the subject at all. The idea is suggested by the advertisement, and the impulsiveness of human nature enforces the suggested idea, hence the desired result follows in a way unknown to the purchaser. (p.175)

Scott also anticipates much later thinking (from James Webb Young and Martin Mayer) about the ways in which advertising adds 'a value not in the product':

...when I think of Ivory Soap, a halo of spotless elegance envelops it, and I do not think of it merely as a prosaic chunk of fat and alkali. I have had this idea of spotless elegance so thoroughly associated with Ivory Soap by means of these many advertisements that I actually enjoy using Ivory Soap more than I should if the soap had not been thus advertised. (p.339)

Scott's language is often rather dated and his opinions of specific ads can be highly subjective. But the refreshing thing about coming to his book after, say, Hopkins or Starch, is that he does come across as genuinely curious about specific advertisements and with an open mind as to the subtlety and complexity of the psychological processes involved. Advertising theory did not start with Hopkins: if anything, his brutal oversimplifications and his enormous subsequent influence had the effect of closing down a much more interesting conversation, rather as Rosser Reeves did again forty years later. In other words, notions of subconscious associations and non-rational suggestion were not invented by Vance Packard's white coated scientists, but have been an accepted way of thinking about advertising since the earliest days: at least, until the imposition of the dogma of rational persuasion and 'reason why' suppressed them.

I think we should accept, then, that psychological theories about the unconscious are unassailably well-founded as a way of understanding advertising effects. We can also accept them as further proof – if we needed it – that the rational persuasion model taken on its own is seriously inadequate. But what, if any, are their limitations?

Over more than a century, writers and theorists such as Scott, Martineau, and Heath have argued with increasing evidence that the rational persuasion model is insufficient and often plain wrong. What is more questionable is how far the 'subconscious' model, in itself, offers practical alternative tools for designing advertising. From Scott's time onwards, the scientists have anticipated a day when persuasion can become, not an art, but a science:

The preparation of copy has usually followed the instincts rather than the analytical functions... But the future must needs be full of better methods than these... the successful advertisers will be likewise termed psychological advertisers. (from an article in *Publicity*, March 1901, quoted in Scott, p.3)

[The ads of the future] will be as effective as the Winchester was against the bow-and-arrow. Why? Because advertisers, when they start to understand the power of Low Attention Processing, will realise that people are vulnerable to implicit learning, and they will use it more and more often. They will seek out markers that are deeply embedded in our minds, and exploit them .... (Heath 2001, p.119)

Yet it seems questionable whether effective advertising is ever created merely by psychological analysis. History suggests that the crucial factors are much more likely to be intuition, imagination, and not infrequently luck. Findings from psychology can offer to post-rationalise how individual campaigns have been effective, but even here they can easily leap from useful insight to highly subjective speculation. I am far from convinced that the kind of white-coated 'hidden persuaders' that Packard evoked can ever be more than a fantasy. At best, psychology can open up new perspectives on a topic that may lead towards something new and powerful, as Dichter often demonstrated – but even in such cases, the psychological 'insight' with hindsight usually appears more as a stepping stone to a new inspiration, rather than a watertight explanation. Does a convertible really have to be a 'mistress' to get men in the show room? Part of the problem with this, of course, is that analysis of what goes on in the subconscious mind is, by definition, impossible: such hypotheses are untestable. All we can say is, in practical terms it was a bright idea that led somewhere new. In general, *post hoc* analyses of ads from either a psychoanalytic or semiotic standpoint fall into this zone of untestability. There was one very eminent, psychoanalytically oriented researcher in the seventies who would argue, for instance, that there were always three men in a lager ad because the number three subconsciously evoked the male genitalia. When this theory was put to John Webster, author of many lager ads himself, he was bemused. 'You can't have one bloke on his own because he'd be a loser; you can't have two in case people think they're gay; you don't want more than three because of the repeat fees.'

So psychological (or semiotic) theories may be valuable in opening up possibilities, and also steering the creative process away from the tramlines of a rational, message transmission approach. I'm more doubtful as to how far they can actually tell us how to design the ads: I don't see much evidence that it's ever been successfully done, and I don't think there's much appetite for it, especially in creative departments. More to the point, it seems unnecessary – countless successful campaigns have worked over the years by being subconsciously processed, but few if any of them were designed in this way. I'd argue that it is the *creative* subconscious, or as we usually call it, intuition or imagination, that chiefly matters. And that may be just as well. Otherwise there would have been a lot more truth in Packard's fears.

Theories about subconscious seduction are then on the one hand, quite compellingly strong. They may be positively helpful in so far as they create legitimacy for the many elements in successful advertising that don't fit the rational persuasion model, going some way at least to explain in general terms the power of music or imagery. But though they may give us permission to value certain things, they don't really tell us how to create powerful advertising.

But is this whole way of thinking just too unnecessarily complicated? Is there a simpler way of explaining the whole phenomenon of advertising – or at least, a large chunk of it? Maybe there is. And the strongest candidate is my next model.

Chapter Twelve:

The Meaningless Distinctive

Advertising as Salience, Fame or 'Mere Publicity'.

Claude Hopkins wrote:

> The purpose of advertising is to sell. It is not to help your other salesmen. It is not to keep your name before the people.

To which I am always tempted to respond – 'Why not, Claude?'. Apart from direct response advertising, 'helping your other salesmen' seems like a much more accurate starting point to describe what most advertising does. And it leads to another helpful maxim, popularised (though not in fact invented) by Stephen King:

> The role of advertising is not so much to increase sales, as to increase saleability.

This notion of saleability is a helpful corrective to the tunnel vision that can be induced by the phrase 'salesmanship in print'. But just now I want to focus on Hopkins's other assertion – 'it is not to keep your name before the people.'

Why did he choose just these words? Because they were already a popular and successful formula used by a rival agency. Hopkins could then position his salesmanship approach as being more sophisticated than this simple principle, and subsequent writers including Reeves would quote the phrase as an example of how primitive advertising was before Hopkins. Yet we may have some strong evidence today that 'keeping your name before the public' – or perhaps more accurately, 'keeping your name in the public mind' – still has a great deal to be said for it.

The case for this has been most persuasively put in recent years by Byron Sharp and other colleagues of the late Andrew Ehrenberg, working for what is now called the Ehrenberg-Bass Institute in Australia. Ehrenberg was an extraordinary man whom I had the privilege to know a little. From the 1950s onwards he carried out a long series of studies which were initially about patterns of buyer behaviour, using panel data. Repeatedly he showed, across all kinds of categories and geographies, that the patterns of brand buying that make up brand shares are remarkably regular and predictable within narrow limits, and also very different from what most conventional marketing theories and most marketers assume. One key finding is that brand size is almost entirely predictable from brand penetration in any given period: average weight of purchase varies very little by brand. This has huge implications for marketing, in that brands cannot grow without attracting more buyers – there is no such thing as a 'niche' brand that is big because a few people buy it with very high frequency. Many people still find this counter-intuitive and refuse to believe it, but I have never seen the data seriously challenged.

Ehrenberg's research also called into question the idea that advertising works by converting buyers from Brand A to Brand B, an assumption that probably has its roots in Claude Hopkins's experience as a travelling preacher. The panel data showed instead that people normally buy a repertoire of brands, and that purchasing loyalty is rare. Ehrenberg developed the idea that advertising principally works by reinforcing existing patterns of buying, and called this the Awareness-Trial-Reinforcement (ATR) model to contrast it with the still popular AIDA. This theory was also a major influence on Stephen King's thinking about brands and the role of advertising.

More recently, the Ehrenberg-Bass people claim to have disproved several other core marketing beliefs. Segmentation is a myth: different brands are bought by essentially the same kinds of people. Brands are not differentiated – attitudes towards different brands in any category are much more similar than they are different. (Ehrenberg would always argue that though some minor variation to these general rules existed, they were much less important than the generalities.) These various findings eventually led Ehrenberg and his colleagues, from about the 1980s on, to argue that the principal way advertising influences buying behaviour is by making brands more salient, that is, more accessible in more consumers' memory. Advertising is therefore, in a phrase they use, 'mere publicity': the role of creativity is neither to persuade nor to seduce, but merely to create images that are closely linked to the brand and which lodge in long term memory. In a powerful expression of Byron Sharp's, advertising does not create meaningful differentiation between brands but 'meaningless distinctiveness' (Sharp, p.112).

Before I offer my own tentative estimate of how adequate this explanation is, I want to add some further strands of evidence or theory that may support it. The first comes from Les Binet and Peter Field's excellent meta-analysis of hundreds of IPA Effectiveness Cases. Binet and Field make two conclusions that seem relevant. They classify campaigns first of all by whether they are emotional, rational, or fame-creating: the most powerful single force is fame. Simply making a brand more famous drives sales. They also confirm a number of previous studies all of which show a strong correlation between a brand's relative Share of Voice and its sales performance: brands that spend above their share of market tend to grow, those that spend less than their share of market tend to decline. While there are obviously exceptions to both these generalities, which perhaps are to be explained by other executional factors, the overall pattern of both sends a clear message: effectively 'keeping your name before the public' is a key factor for advertising success.

Why might it be the case that people tend to prefer and choose the brands that are most 'top of mind'? There are a number of possibilities from the literature of psychology or behavioural economics. One is the relation between what psychologists have labelled 'mere exposure' and 'affect' – or as Robert Cialdini sums it up in his book *Influence*, 'For the most part, we like things that are familiar to us'. Then, the so-called 'availability heuristic', written about by Daniel Kahneman and others, states that things we think of first or can picture most vividly are assumed to be most common and important. Applied to brands, this implies that people assume the brand that comes to mind first is likely to be the biggest and most popular. And that in turn provides the reassurance that Cialdini labels as 'social proof' – we are reassured not just by our own familiarity with a brand name, but by the assumption that many others also use it. Jim Crimmins and Ned Anschuetz, my colleagues at DDB Chicago, showed many years ago across the world and across all categories, that the biggest brands had higher proportions of emotionally loyal users than smaller brands: this was not what they had expected. They attributed this counter-intuitive finding to similar psychological principles: that people most value and are most attached to what they perceive others as valuing.

It's worth noticing here that virtually all the discourses of both rational persuasion and subconscious seduction tend to conceptualise the advertising process as a one to one communication between brand and individual consumer – a conceptualisation that carries through to most conventional ad testing techniques. However, it may be very important to consider that the effects of advertising are to a significant extent social. Preference for a brand will be influenced by seeing others use it, by the conversations we share about it, or merely by the perception that a brand is popular with others – a perception which advertising of sufficient ubiquity may help to create. This would at least be consistent with Binet and Field's finding that sheer weight of advertising relative to brand share tends to lead to growth. And the importance of understanding brand behaviour in social terms rather than individual has in recent years been emphasised by Mark Earls in his work on the Herd mentality.

All of this evidence suggests that simply being famous, appearing to be ubiquitous and popular, are in themselves important factors in building brands – and that this may be a major function of advertising. My personal feeling is that the Ehrenberg-Sharp theory, when it implies that this is all that advertising does, overstates the case. The theory leaves too much out, and is just *too* simple on its own. But I also want to stress that I think it accounts for an awful lot of what advertising does, and its importance is generally much underestimated by practitioners. Many advertisers could probably do a great deal better than they do now if they simply followed the precepts of fame, mere publicity, and equilibrium share of voice with energy and consistency. At this level, advertising isn't rocket science, and those advertisers who behave as if it were, who try to be too clever and are too anxious about getting it wrong, generally handicap themselves by producing campaigns that are inconsistent, timid, over-analysed and under-resourced. Against this, the consistent application of the 'meaningless distinctive' will I am certain generally win. The only thing against it is that it doesn't make anyone look particularly clever – not the client, certainly not the planners, and not even the creative department – so nobody usually wants to do it.

Chapter Thirteen:

It's Like Love

Advertising as Social Connection – Watzlawick and Communication Theory

ntil the 1960s, theories of communication focused only on the transmission of messages: sophisticated theories about 'signal' and 'noise', but essentially an engineering approach. (Is it coincidence that Rosser Reeves's thinking about advertising similarly focused on message transmission?) Then a multidisciplinary group of thinkers, sometimes known as 'The Invisible College' or 'The Palo Alto School' after the Californian city where they were centred, shifted the foundations of communication theory in ways that were ahead of their time (Mattelart and Mattelart, pp.51-3). The member of this group whose thinking I want to concentrate on here was a psychotherapist called Paul Watzlawick.

As a therapist, Watzlawick must have observed continually that communication – for instance between warring spouses – meant much more than whether a simple 'message' was transmitted or not. The more interesting questions for Watzlawick became – what constitutes communication? what role does communication play in our lives? His answers to such questions are both, in one sense, obvious, and yet also totally radical because they invite us to think about communication in a completely different way. And I think that way has some very valuable implications for how we can choose to think about advertising. I can summarise most of Watzlawick's key thinking by using some of his own 'five axioms' which structure his 1967 book, *Pragmatics of Human Communication*.

The first axiom is: it is impossible not to communicate. In other words, we don't just communicate when we choose to speak or send out a message; in fact, we don't only communicate when we *intend* to communicate. You can see the truth of this if you consider, for example, how you might interpret someone else's failure to return a phone call – especially if they were a lover, say, or a client. Or if you and I have a friendly working relationship, then one day we pass in the street and I say nothing and avoid your gaze. In both cases, there might or might not have been an intention to communicate, yet the other will almost certainly interpret what happens as having meaning. Everything, then, is communication – not just speech or silence, but body language, dress, behaviour, context.... This idea alone has huge and fairly clear implications for brands, and also for individual advertisements. It emphasises again that we do not just respond to the intended 'message' of an ad, but to every detail of it – and possibly in ways that were not intended.

The second axiom acknowledges that communication does not take place as a single, one way transmission but is a continual exchange. My failure to say hello when we pass in the street only has its meaning for you because of our previous history of communication, and will influence what happens next: perhaps next time we meet you will respond in turn by ignoring me, or alternatively will make a special effort to appear friendly. And what's happening in this series of exchanges is the all important subject of a third axiom – all communication is not just about content, but about relationship. Let's examine that a bit further.

Why, after all, did we have a previous custom of speaking when we met? It would be rare that we had anything substantive to say to each other. Perhaps we would often talk, as people do, about the weather, but not usually because one of us knew something that the other didn't. 'Bit colder this morning' – 'Yes, I must get my winter coat out'. Like much conversation, this isn't really about the content at all. What it is really saying, in the words of Watzlawick's colleague Gregory Bateson, is something more like 'We are not enemies'.

Of course, in much verbal communication the content may be rather more significant than this: but it is never the *only* thing that is going on. The ways in which we interact, the words we choose to say or not to say, the way in which we say them, the ways we look and stand and sit, the clothes we wear, the gestures we make (for instance, offering to pay for lunch, asking for help), are all as we have seen 'communication' and all are continually constructing, maintaining, or changing our relationship. Again, this is radical thinking, but once you start to notice it, it may come to seem obvious. (Watzlawick himself illustrates the principle, quite entertainingly, in his book, by analysing the dialogue from Edward Albee's great play about a dysfunctional marriage, *Who's Afraid of Virginia Woolf?*)

There's one more key idea that Watzlawick adds to this. He draws a distinction between two modes of communication, which he calls the digital and the analogic. Remember he was writing in the 1960s and the word 'digital' didn't have a lot of the baggage it does for us today. We can get his point most easily perhaps by thinking of digital versus analogue clock faces. A digital time display (like the one on my computer) shows time as numbers; the analogue face on my wrist shows time in a spatial way, by how far a needle has passed around a circle. These are so visually different that a person unfamiliar with timekeeping would never guess they served the same function. The digital face is both abstract and precise: the numbers 8:18 only mean something to me because I interpret them, but they tell me exactly what the time is. The analogue face is a gesture which I have to interpret in quite a different way – even if I don't know exactly what the time is, I can see spatially that the big hand is about a third of the way round (so it's *roughly* twenty past the hour), and if I'm waiting for something, I can watch it impatiently as it moves.

On this model, what Watzlawick means by digital communication is any message with content that is finite, replicable, and precise. 'Meet me under the clock at Paddington at half past two'. 'Like for like sales in Q3 were 674,000.' 'I fed the cat this morning'. Even statements such as these will very likely also have a relationship aspect that is quite separate from the content, and it's not hard to imagine many different possibilities for what these might be – they would, of course, be context dependent. (Suppose Sir Alan Sugar is telling you the sales figures, you're the sales manager, and the figure is half what he expected...) But the content, at least, is fairly unambiguous.

Analogic communication on the other hand is less precise, more gestural, more ambiguous. It may be verbal – 'Starless and Bible Black', 'What are you doing that for?' 'Get lost'. Or it may be non-verbal: a facial expression, a physical gesture, a touch, a shrug, wearing a tie for a meeting... any of which in context may evoke a powerful effect, but depend on interpretation. (And in the words of G.H.Mead, 'the meaning of a gesture is given by the response'.)

And this analogic mode of communication is extremely important; because according to Watzlawick, it is the analogic level of communication that primarily influences relationships.

Now Watzlawick was not thinking at all about advertising when he wrote all this – his main focus was on his work as a therapist, and his theories have other important applications. I strongly suspect that he didn't even like advertising very much and wouldn't be delighted to think that he'd helped it in any way. But, like it or not, advertising is an aspect of human communication, and I think he offers us another way of thinking about advertising that may be very practical.

First of all it shifts our focus away from the *content* of the advertising – which generally obsesses everyone's attention – and invites us to think instead about what the advertising is doing, and what we want it to do, for the *relationship* between the brand and the consumer. It also reframes advertising as not just a one-way, message transmission relationship , but as a continuing exchange. It may be, of course, that the consumer's part in the exchange mainly consists of buying or not buying the brand, though it may well also involve more complex interactions: such as dealings with sales staff, conversations with other consumers, and today also interactions online, and the use of social media. Watzlawick also makes clear that everything a brand does is potentially communication, and everything in an ad is also communication – restating in a different way Stephen King's argument that an ad works as a whole, and is not separable into 'message' and 'execution'. And if we see the primary function of the ad now as influencing the nature of the relationship between consumer and brand, Watzlawick tells us that it is the analogic aspects of that communication that will mainly do this. In other words, it is the tone of voice, the detail of the execution, the connotative use of language, *all things that conventional advertising theory has treated as peripheral,* that are in fact the most important.

And here's the kicker: Watzlawick makes it very clear that it is *impossible* to translate the analogic aspects of communication into digital terms. We can try, but we will always ultimately fail. It is therefore precisely the aspects of an ad that are most important in making it effective that most defy our attempts to analyse them or put them into words. To say that this is an uncomfortable thought for most organisations (and researchers) is an understatement. Watzlawick's theory supports Bill Bernbach's many sayings on this matter, such as

It's like love – the more you analyse it, the more it disappears.

or

How do you storyboard a smile?

Advertisers often hamper their own work by insisting that they will only run advertising that they can explain in a logical way. This demand accounts for the continuing dominance of the supposedly rational, proposition based models. But looked at through the lens of Watzlawick's theory of human communication, this is absurd. It is a bit like trying to make friends with someone by preparing ever more clever things to say about the weather, while forgetting to smile.

I invite you to apply Watzlawick's thinking to whatever campaigns you admire and know to have been successful; I think you will find that the advertising is most easily understood as a series of gestures intended to create a relationship. One example I have often used to illustrate this point is a famous, creatively lauded and highly effective campaign from the Netherlands for an insurance company called Centraal Beheer. Over more than two decades, this brand has achieved and held on to leadership in its category with a series of commercials that are in effect sixty second comedies. They are exquisitely filmed with high production values and assume considerable intelligence in the audience. (You should be able to find them on YouTube). The connection with insurance is slight: each film ends with an unexpected disaster, and the only mention of the brand is in an end frame with the words 'Just call us'. From the point of view of proposition advertising, it makes little sense; indeed, many professionals seeing these films for the first time suspect they must be a bit of pure creative indulgence. Yet the campaign is undoubtedly effective, and has won awards for effectiveness as well as creativity.

You could explain the success of this campaign through the 'mere publicity' theory: they spend enough, they get noticed, they become top of mind. I couldn't say that's wrong. But I find the relationship view more satisfying. Part of the background to this brand is that they launched when insurance was still mainly bought in the Netherlands through a broker – someone the family would have a personal relationship with. One of the important things this campaign has done right from the start is creating a similar friendly relationship with a brand that sells direct. Insurance is a dull subject, so simply appearing on television with some factual claims might not be enough to compete with the friendly family broker. Instead, Centraal Beheer chose to invite themselves into the living room (as Martin Boase would have said) with a present – sixty seconds of high class entertainment – that would make people smile and be glad to see them return. The TV advertising was the start of a beautiful friendship.

Incidentally, Centraal Beheer also do direct response advertising that actually sells – and it's as dull and factual as Claude Hopkins could ever have dreamt of. The effectiveness studies show clearly that these two approaches work in harmony. The TV creates the friendly relationship; the print gets on with the practical detail and closes the sale. But without the relationship being maintained, response to the selling ads can be shown to drop off quite quickly. Or as Stephen King would have put it – the TV creates saleability, the print creates the sales.

I wouldn't argue that this way of looking at advertising is all that is necessary. Human communication is more complex than that, and for the desired relationship to take place the advertiser may need to do many things – to give information, to be repetitive, to sell hard, as well as to charm or entertain. But I suggest that 'relationship' is always a useful way of thinking about any campaign, and may often turn out to be the one that makes most practical sense. You could argue that all the great ad professionals of the past did this intuitively. When Hopkins advised against humour, he was aiming to construct a certain relationship, that with a trustworthy seller: Reeves's ads created a relationship based on a brash confidence and authority; Ogilvy's impressed by snob appeal. And the DDB tone of voice, radical in its day, was based entirely on a particular kind of conversation with the consumer. They could so easily have said something like 'Nine out of ten snowplow drivers use a Volkswagen!' What they chose to say instead, of course, was 'Have you ever wondered.....?'

That is the difference between the digital and analogic modes. And the difference lies not in the content, but in the relationship that is created.

Chapter Fourteen:

Without the Prod of Salesmanship

Advertising as Spin: Edward Bernays and the Story of Public Relations

The next idea is to consider advertising as influencing the construction of a shared reality.

This may sound another rather theoretical idea and I could indeed support it from a theoretical perspective such as social constructionism. But in a brief sketch I'm coming at it from a much more tangible strand of history – the world of public relations, or, as it's become popularly and rather unkindly known, Spin.

It's only quite recently that I've started to find out much about the history of PR and I've discovered a world which is a strange parallel to that of advertising – with both some similarities and some important differences. *The central figure in the story of PR is Edward Bernays – he's by no means the only one, but he was so influential that you might say he was the Hopkins, Reeves, Dichter and Bernbach of the PR world. It helped that he lived to over a hundred, and was still working actively in his hundredth* year. Like Ernest Dichter, he was born an Austrian Jew - he was Sigmund Freud's double nephew - but he grew up and studied in the USA. Graduating from Cornell in 1913, he became editor of a medical magazine, where he published an article about a French play called *Damaged Goods*, a highly controversial piece about syphilis which at the time was not openly discussed. Knowing that *Damaged Goods* would have difficulty being shown in New York, where the guardians of public morals would almost certainly close it down, Bernays offered his support to the producer. He then came up with the following cunning plan. In his role as editor he established a new organisation, the Medical Review's Sociological Fund Committee. Its stated objective was to advance public instruction about venereal diseases. Bernays then invited many of New York's elite to donate and join the committee, including the Rockefellers and the Vanderbilts. Only after the committee was established, was it suggested to the members that it could advance its aims by supporting the production of *Damaged Goods* in New York. The plan worked like a charm. The play received enthusiastic coverage, was supported by President Wilson himself, went on tour and was made into a film. Soon afterwards Bernays left his editing job and set himself up under the newly coined title of 'Counsel on Public Relations'.

What Bernays did with *Damaged Goods* is indicative of some of the principles he continued to work with throughout his career. His approach is the antithesis of direct persuasion or confrontation: indeed, there's a distinct air of working both behind the scenes and in a roundabout way. Neither the public, nor even the committee, would have suspected that there was any 'manipulation' involved. What Bernays had so cleverly done was to redefine the terms in which the play was viewed (what in behavioural economics is called 'framing'). On its own it would have been seen merely as 'shocking prurient play from Paris' and the puritanical powers of New York would have had no trouble closing it down, with support from the public and probably the very people that Bernays had invited on to his committee. By setting up the responsibly and boringly named Medical Review's Sociological Fund Committee, Bernays reframed the play as part of a worthy, even dull, public health education project. This may be as good an example as any of what I mean when I talk about the construction of a shared reality. Suddenly everyone saw *Damaged Goods* in a completely different way – and weren't even aware they had been influenced to do so.

Bernays's preferred *modus operandi* was always, where possible, to remain invisible. He disdained the term 'press agent' and claimed he never needed to ask editors for help: instead he helped to create news events and stories which they could not resist covering. Bernays and the other key figures in PR also understood all the principles that I've applied to advertising in this book, although the giving of facts or information was usually the least important to them. Indeed Bernays repeatedly says this is *not* how public relations works:

> Abstract discussions and heavy facts... cannot be given to the public until they are simplified and dramatized.(Ewen, p.170)

The public are to be influenced, on the contrary, through their emotions, through the power of story, and above all through the visual image. Bernays was also well aware of the already established theory of the 'herd instinct', and had used it in the case of *Damaged Goods*: if you can get the leaders of the herd to move one way, the rest will follow. As Freud's nephew, he also entirely took for granted the importance of unconscious motivations:

> Men are rarely aware of the real reasons which motivate their action... many of man's thoughts and actions are compensatory substitutes for desires which he has been obliged to suppress. (Bernays, pp.74-5)

Public Relations also understood well the notion of creating a relationship. The whole presidency of Franklin D. Roosevelt was a triumph of well managed PR, largely down to the natural talents of FDR himself. During his presidency he gave a long series of 'fireside chats' on national radio, in which he managed to achieve the tone of an intimate friend speaking to each family in the land individually, in their own home. One commentator who had watched his audiences described them thus:

> I have sat in those parlors and on those porches myself during some of the speeches, and I have seen men and women gathered around the radio, even those who didn't like him or were opposed to him politically, listening with a pleasant, happy feeling of association and friendship....(Ewen, p.254)

So PR from the 1920s on knew all the tricks of advertising, and had fewer hang-ups about practising them. But fundamental to it all, I think, was a bigger notion: that public opinion, culture, the world of meanings that we share, is not absolute but always there to be influenced – and that if you don't influence it yourself, others will. Bernays never saw himself as disguising the truth; he saw himself as shaping the truth. The pioneers of PR such as Bernays were quite unashamed of this view because they genuinely believed that their interventions were for the best. Perhaps most people would agree that showing *Damaged Goods* was 'a good thing'; many would still argue that Roosevelt's New Deal (which was enabled by PR) was a 'good thing'. But of course in the world of politics and power one group's 'good thing' may be very much another group's 'bad thing'. Even Bernays had to admit that the tools of PR could be used for evil purposes as well as good, and it is said that Joseph Goebbels was a great fan of Bernays's 1929 book, *Propaganda*. All this is undeniable, and arguably many of the ills of today's society have been exacerbated if not created by the use of PR in their own interests by powerful bodies. Yet there remains the counter argument that whatever you believe, you have got to use the tools of PR if you want to achieve your goals; and few organisations have ever used PR more effectively to further their own belief systems than ecological lobby groups such as Friends of the Earth or Greenpeace.

How useful is it then to think of advertising as another device for constructing a shared reality? I think at a deep level it's all pervasive. Let's take Lynx/Axe as a good example. The original product was a deodorant: the advertising has entirely reframed this, not merely as a fragrance, but as an aid to seduction. (Actually I suspect the real benefit is confidence, but that's a discussion for another time.) Advertising alone has created a reality in which clothes are presumed to require fabric conditioner in order to be pleasant to touch. Volkswagen in the 1960s took an odd looking, tiny car and reframed it as economical, sturdy and practical.

The principal difference is that while PR aspires ideally to become invisible, advertising by definition can't be – it always appears in some sort of a frame which is explicitly labelled 'advertisement'. Yet at another level what advertising does is often, as they say, 'hidden in plain view'. We may all see Cheryl Cole in the L'Oreal ad and consciously ridicule it; but as Bernays knew, the public is not immune to an image in the same way they might be immune to an argument. Endlessly repeated, L'Oreal advertising consistently reinforces our shared unspoken beliefs about what is beautiful hair, what women should look like, our relationship with celebrity, L'Oreal's own power and dominance in the field - and the fact that science is important even if we don't expect to understand it.

As Mark Crispin Miller puts it in his (2005) introduction to *Propaganda*: '[Bernays's] aim was... to *transform the buyer's very world*, so that the product must appear to be desirable as if without the prod of salesmanship' (Bernays, p.19, emphasis added). Advertising often achieves this too.

Chapter Fifteen:

Din and Tinsel

Advertising as Showmanship: P. T. Barnum and the Art of Humbug

Before there was Claude Hopkins, before there was Edward Bernays, before there was Walter Dill Scott, there was Phineas T. Barnum.

Barnum was born in Connecticut in 1810. He began his long career as a showman and impresario in 1835 by exhibiting an infirm 80 year old black woman, Joyce Heth, with the claim that she was 160 years old and had been George Washington's nurse. He followed the success of this with the 'Feejee Mermaid', a fairly shameless hoax made from the remains of a monkey and a fish, and 'General Tom Thumb', a four year old dwarf whom Barnum claimed was eleven. Barnum later went into more respectable theatrical shows where he made many successful innovations, such as reserved seats and matinee performances. In 1850 he promoted a worldwide tour of the celebrated Swedish soprano, Jenny Lind, and in his sixties he developed the celebrated three ring circus for which he is still perhaps best remembered, the 'greatest show on earth' for which he bought Jumbo the elephant from London Zoo. He died in 1891.

What makes Barnum remarkable and historically important was his enormous flair as a publicist, and his ability to create public interest in his attractions on a massive, even global scale. For this he is sometimes said to be the originator of modern mass media culture. For Barnum there was no such thing as bad publicity – he revelled in the controversies about whether his exhibits were real or fakes, often deliberately deceiving his customers one way or another. He never took himself entirely seriously, yet was candidly devoted to making money. He was also a great self-publicist, and wrote about himself throughout his career, sometimes lampooning himself as 'Barnaby Diddleum'. All that mattered for Barnum was to keep his name before the public – and where have we heard that before? – and ensure that people in their thousands continued to talk about, argue about, and turn up for his shows. His favourite word for what he did was 'humbug'.

In his 1864 book, *Ancient and Modern Humbugs of the World*, Barnum makes it clear exactly what he means by this term. He does *not* mean swindling, although a certain kind of deception may be very excellent humbug if it draws the crowds – as long as they decide in the end they are getting value for their money. He describes Monsieur Mangin, 'the French Humbug', who made a fortune selling pencils in Paris by dint of pure entertainment and showmanship, and described his secret as follows: 'First, attract the public by din and tinsel, by brilliant sky-rockets and Bengola lights, then give them as much as possible for their money.' (Cook, p.91). Barnum himself explains it as follows: '"humbug" consists in putting on glittering appearances – outside show – novel expedients, by which to suddenly arrest public attention, and attract the public eye and ear... An honest man who thus arrests public attention will be called a "humbug", but he is not a swindler or an impostor.' (Cook, p.95) For Barnum, there may be humbug in all walks of life, and he argues that it is the only key to success – those who disdain to employ it, however good their product, will never get rich.

Having spent quite a long time now examining theories of advertising which claim it is either based on sober factual arguments, or complicated depth psychology, or other abstract principles, I found myself happily seduced by Barnum and his talk of humbug. Running throughout this discussion has been a continual question – is advertising a science or an art?

Many people have wanted it to be a science, for all sorts of reasons. And there are certainly aspects where a scientific approach can tell us much, whether it's the rigorous empirical analysis of sales responses, or of patterns of buyer behaviour, or our ever increasing understanding of perception, memory, and decision-making, through psychology, sociology, and neuroscience. Yet outside some narrow limits science has proven to be an unsatisfactory tool for actually creating effective campaigns.

Art too has a lot to offer; it proposes an alternative set of values based on aesthetics, the importance of imagination, the power of originality, an approach to communication that utilises the full spectrum of human consciousness, not just the logical rational stratum on the surface of it. And I think Bernbach was largely right when he said that persuasion is not a science, but an art. It's just that 'art' often seems rather too grand a word for what advertising does, and perhaps after all it would be more helpful to think of it as something a little less hifalutin – not so much salesmanship, as showmanship. So while advertising has claims in part to be science, and in part to be art, perhaps its strongest claim – though it has frequently disdained it – is to be humbug.

Humbug, as Barnum promotes it, is about shamelessly rigging the odds in your favour. It's going with your gut feeling. It's sticking your neck out and not worrying too much what others might think. It believes that there's no such thing as bad publicity. It's not ashamed to be popular, vulgar, even crass. It doesn't take itself too seriously, but it also knows that if it doesn't get enough people in the tent, it won't eat. It's confident and has a brass neck.

And this principle of humbug fits surprisingly well with much of what has succeeded best in the world of advertising. Let's take William Hesketh Lever as an early example, the flamboyant nineteenth century entrepreneur who built his soap empire partly on the power of publicity. Lever's ads ranged from the detailed 'reason why' long copy approach, to adapted fine art paintings of cute children and animals. (And when one aggrieved artist tried to sue him, the resulting publicity kept Lever laughing all the way to the bank.) Unconstrained by any theories of advertising, he went with his instincts and advanced on all fronts. In the 1890s he published the Sunlight Year book, an annual reference work and guide to life which was given away free to schools and to users who saved enough Sunlight cartons – something we should now grandly call 'sponsored content'. In 1887 Lever Bros. announced that it would give £2000 to the 'religious and benevolent institution' that most customers voted for (votes on the back of a Sunlight box only) – what we should now call 'Cause Related Marketing'. When the RNLI won, he presented them with a lifeboat, called 'Sunlight Number One', and then commissioned engravings of it in a choppy sea, the name plate highly prominent, which he sent to the *Illustrated London News*. For the first London to Brighton car run in 1896, celebrating the end to the rule that a man with a red flag should walk in front of every vehicle, he entered three vans blazoned with Sunlight ads – they set off ten hours early, at midnight, and the *Daily Mail* printed the story under the headline 'Sunlight at Midnight'. He used sponsorship, product placement, and so on.....there was nothing Bernays could have taught Lever about making news, though there may well have been something that Lever learnt from Barnum.

By the early twentieth century, Barnum was already becoming a figure that the advertising industry wanted to distance itself from, as it aspired to professionalism, science, and higher purpose. With his ballyhoo, cheerful vulgarity and casual attitude to 'truth', he became a sort of embarrassing mad uncle, disowned and locked in the attic (Marchand, pp.7-8).

Yet I think each of the other main protagonists in my story – Hopkins, Bernays, Reeves, Dichter, Ogilvy, Bernbach – fundamentally based his success and his clients' successes on a solid foundation of humbug, however they may have tried to disguise it as something more respectable. If you look at what Hopkins actually did – and less at what he wrote in *Scientific Advertising* – he too was pretty good at humbug. You'll remember perhaps, from an earlier chapter, 'the biggest cake in the world' which he produced for Cotosuet, and displayed in a Chicago department store; police had to hold back the crowds. There are other examples in his interesting autobiography, *My Life in Advertising*.

What Bernays did - including the way he dignified his own role as either a 'doctor' or a 'counsel' on public relations – is often pure humbug, and Barnum would have recognised a fellow master of the art. The chief difference between the two is that while Barnum's stunts always put Barnum in the spotlight, Bernays preferred to remain invisible. And while he typically claimed his methods were more scientific and sophisticated than Barnum's, he still grudgingly acknowledged the importance of his predecessor:

> The business man and advertising man is realizing that he must not discard entirely the methods of Barnum in reaching the public. (Bernays, p.101)

In 1929 he orchestrated a worldwide media celebration, 'Light's Golden Jubilee', to celebrate the fiftieth anniversary of Edison's invention of the light bulb – though only a few insiders would have suspected this was anything other than a spontaneous tribute. There was a US commemorative postage stamp; feature articles in all the leading magazines; George M. Cohan wrote a song, 'Edison-Miracle Man', whose music was distributed around the world. All this however was but the prelude to the centrepiece event on October 21, when at Dearborn,

Michigan, an ancient Thomas Edison publicly appeared to switch on a replica of his first light bulb in the presence of President Hoover, Marie Curie, Orville Wright, and other notables; his act was then repeated in nations around the world, as people turned on their lights in a moment of planetary togetherness. None of this, of course, had happened by accident: it was all arranged by Bernays, as paid impresario for General Electric, as part of a wider agenda to change public perceptions of big business from exploiters to benefactors of humanity.

I claim that Dichter, Reeves, Bernbach, and Ogilvy were all talented humbugs, both on behalf of their clients *and* on behalf of themselves. Bernbach is particularly interesting. Before working in advertising, he had been part of the publicity team behind the 1939 New York World's Fair – like Light's Golden Jubilee ten years earlier, this was on the face of it an entertainment and a celebration of Roosevelt's New Deal, yet in reality an opportunity for big corporations to vindicate themselves in the public mind by taking the credit for improvements in Americans' standard of living. Bernbach's assumption of authority in adland may have been helped by the fact that he thought as much like a PR man as an ad man:

We are so busy measuring public opinion that we forget we can mould it.

All of us who professionally use the mass media are the shapers of society. We can vulgarize that society. We can brutalize it. Or we can help lift it onto a higher level.

As I drew towards the end of writing this chapter, occasionally taking a break to look at Facebook, the latest 'viral' commercial kept popping up on my friends' pages. It showed two huge Volvo trucks, driving backwards together in parallel, while between them a famous film actor, Jean-Claude Van Damme – actually, very much in the character of the old style circus strong man or acrobat – stands between them on their wing mirrors and slowly, dramatically, does the splits.

Now I think we could explain this commercial to our satisfaction in any one of the six models I've talked about. There is a rational proposition – these trucks have superior steering. There is subconscious association – they're tough and handsome like the actor. There's fame – it's just getting talked about. And so on.

But when I saw this commercial, my first thought was – this is straight out of the fairground. It's pure P.T.Barnum. This is pure humbug.

And there's nothing wrong with that, nothing wrong with that at all.

Epilogue

Though we want ideas, we haven't learnt how to handle them. We use them up too quickly. We get rid of them by immediately putting them into practice.....

Therefore, in what follows I shall not be elaborating direct applications for business organizations and their managerial conundrums. I worry lest the birds be caged too soon.

James Hillman, *Kinds of Power*, pp.18-19

Epilogue

eflecting on the history of advertising thought has led me to realise that there is much more possible diversity in ways of thinking about advertising than we normally allow, and that we could use this diversity to give us greater scope in what we do. For all its talk of 'creativity' and 'thinking outside the box', the ad business today is in sad danger of losing its diversity. Creative people and marketing people alike each go to the same schools, learn the same things, and the same things they learn are too often a third-hand mash-up of Reeves's USP theory and Bernbach's vague creative rhetoric. But in creating ads, we still have the full resources of human culture at our disposal. Ads don't need to look as if they were written by Bernbach sixty years ago, or like last year's Cannes winner.

Any one of the six ways of thinking described here can open up exciting possibilities for us in any given situation, if we allow ourselves to be open to it. (And I repeat, there is nothing magical about these six perspectives, or the number six. I can already think of two or three others that might have an equal right to be included, and so perhaps can you.) Conversely, if we apply any one dogmatically as a set of rules, it closes down possibilities, and ultimately may make our work impossible: and unfortunately, this is too often how the past has been used by advertisers. Only take the past as a rich source of inspiration, and it will feed you. I have been inspired by reading about what our predecessors in this profession did, as well as what they wrote; it's striking that none of them, in practice, felt constrained by their own rules.

I also want to acknowledge that there are a great number of important figures I have left out: Stanley and Helen Resor, Theodore MacManus, Leo Burnett, Raymond Rubicam, Bruce Barton, Howard Gossage... the list, as copywriters used to say, is endless. My only excuse for these glaring omissions is that I believe our inherited traditions of advertising thinking have been disproportionately influenced by those who wrote the books, rather than by those who just made ads. Hopkins and Reeves weren't necessarily the greatest ad makers of all time, but they wrote the best-selling books – and as I've suggested, what they wrote doesn't even represent their own practice accurately. Despite that, what they wrote has provided the language and structure of the industry's mental landscape, to an extraordinary degree in a business that traditionally doesn't value book-learning.

I do urge you to go back to the history for yourselves. Stephen Fox's *The Mirror Makers* or Martin Mayer's *Madison Avenue USA* would be very good places to start. I think you will be amazed by what you find, a rich and provocative set of characters and opinions that this short summary of mine has done little justice to. Again, we could liberate ourselves by learning to read the past appreciatively, as a source of inspiration, rather than as a source of rules and precedents.

*

There's a temptation for me, in this final section, to start spelling out the practical implications of these ideas. I could, perhaps, attempt to offer you a Ten Point Plan or Seven Core Principles; perhaps some of you are even hoping I will.

I am going to resist this temptation. In years of teaching and lecturing I learnt to recognise and, eventually, to resist the moment when the audience's demands for me to solve all its problems in advance became overwhelming. 'But what do we do if...?' 'What if the client disagrees?' 'I have just one more *little* question...'. Well, I've given you what I've given you; it's now up to you to decide what to do with it in the messy reality of your own situation. My only advice, for what it's worth, is this. Don't be in too much of a hurry to change the world – you are unlikely to succeed. And when you fail, you'll be tempted to reject all the crazy ideas in this book as impractical and impossible. You are, of course, free to reject them. But I encourage you not to do that too quickly. Go on living with them. Criticise them and argue with them by all means. Develop them into something better if you can. And maybe then, in ways that neither you nor I can plan or predict, some things may start to shift in how you work. In the words of the Jungian analyst, James Hillman:

My idea about ideas is that they first need to be *entertained*. Then they may spark better ones in your mind and can lead to unforeseeable implementation in your life. p.19

However, there is just one strand of thought that I want to pursue a bit further before I close. It was triggered by a discussion at BBH, when someone observed that I hadn't said a lot about the past, or the future, of advertising media. I'd like to say a little about it now.

A lot of the advertising industry's attention today (2014) is focused on the continuing developments in media channels; most obviously the growth of the internet and the ways it can be accessed, and within that mobile and 'social media'. It would be foolish to pretend these are not significant developments, if only because of their enormous scale and the vast sums of money involved. Much commentary around this is ill-informed, as when we hear that television is no longer important, or that the ability of online media to target individuals makes broadcast media obsolete. Television, up to the time of writing at any rate, continues to grow in importance in both developed and developing markets; and even if the targeting accuracy of the internet lived up to its hype (which I'm not convinced it does), it wouldn't replace the need to communicate publicly with mass populations, as Byron Sharp, Les Binet and Peter Field have convincingly argued.

Nevertheless, the future continues to evolve in surprising ways which none of us can predict. 'Television' in the broad sense of audio-visual content seems likely to retain its power as a medium, though the ways it is accessed are already changing fast and will probably have implications for advertising eventually, if not very soon. I personally shudder at most descriptions of the 'internet of things', but I can't assume it won't happen in some form. Indeed, if you're reading this even a few years after I wrote it, you'll probably be aware of changes that make even my most guarded comments seem naive.

So this is undoubtedly a time of great change in the media available to advertisers and marketers. More arguable, however, is whether these changes are more or less significant than those of the previous century. Since the time of P.T.Barnum, the ad business has seen the advent at various times of mass circulation periodicals, colour printing, mass reproduction of photography, massive increases in literacy, an efficient postal service, many different ways to transfer money safely at a distance, the telegraph, the telegram, cinematic projection, sound recording, 'talking pictures', broadcast radio, television, colour television, and associated with most of these, huge developments in popular culture. It is arguable that any of these had an impact on advertising at least as important as the advent of the internet.

These changes in the media landscape must have been a significant influence on the development of advertising thinking as I have sketched it in this book. For examples, the growth of 'direct response' and long copy was partly fuelled by mass literacy, widely available periodicals, and the split run; the Starch rating, and its consequent emphasis on 'attention', worked for an era dominated by mass circulation colour magazines; Rosser Reeves's obsession with the correct recall of a 'selling proposition' was a response to the new medium of broadcast television. To some extent, then, changes in the fashion of thinking about advertising have been led by changes in the dominant media channels. And today, it seems probable that those fashions are similarly being led by the internet – with its emphasis on measurement, targeting and clicks.

My purpose in writing this book, however, is to urge advertising professionals not to allow their thinking, or their imagination, to be constrained by what happens to be fashionable. The reality is that these various implicit models, theories or belief systems about advertising – salesmanship, seduction, showmanship and so on - exist independently of any particular medium and of any particular time. They are all available as resources for all time. You can use printed text, online or offline, to carry a list of product features, a personal letter, or a poem. Thirty seconds (or thirty minutes) of audio-visual can be a lecture, a documentary, or a scene from *Apocalypse Now*. New technology has simply added, and will continue to add, to the array of media choices available to the advertiser, but within any of those media you can choose to be Bernbach, Bernays, or Barnum. You can put the Biggest Cake in the World in a shop window open to millions, or you can set out your counter and have a one to one dialogue with your customer. You can think about what you're doing as factual persuasion, artistic seduction, the creation of subconscious associations, the nurturing of a relationship, or just 'keeping your name before the public' – and no doubt many other things too. Including, and by no means least, humbug.

You are free to think differently.

Appendices
& Bibliography

Appendix 1:

Where do academic theories of advertising fit in?

Since the time of Walter Dill Scott, the amount of academic attention paid to advertising has grown and grown – predominantly in the US, but more recently in Europe and now also in Asia. Academic study of advertising can in principle come from a range of disciplines, but probably the main two have been economics and, most of all, behavioural science or psychology. The principal theme of academic advertising research has always been the not unreasonable sounding quest for a coherent and empirically based body of theory that will help (or even direct) more successful advertising practice. To that end, many thousands of clever people have lent their energy and intellect; professors have been tenured, PhD theses written, and thousands of papers published in peer-reviewed journals. The scale of the effort involved is impressive.

How far has this quest to determine a sound and practical theoretical basis for advertising practice succeeded? This is a difficult and perhaps even a dangerous question to attempt an answer to. I suspect that on the one hand there is much useful learning buried in the academic discourse which practitioners might benefit from understanding. On the other hand, the goal of a coherent body of academic theory that makes any sense of the daily reality of advertising, let alone offers practical guidelines to doing it better, still feels to me very remote – though I think this may be more to do with the unrealistic nature of the quest than the failings of those who have been pursuing it. As with practitioner theory, I have the idea that academic research may be valuable and useful to practice when it opens up new possibilities, gets us out of our ruts, and gives us confidence to follow our intuitions. But when it attempts to prescribe its own set of rules (which are never uncontested) it tends to become a deadening influence. The Quest for Certainty and the creation of highly effective advertising are mutually incompatible.

Although the worlds of advertising practice and advertising academe are separate, they are connected. I hypothesise that there are two main conduits between them. The first is the teaching of business schools and the theories and textbooks that they use, which represent a potentially important influence on the thinking of business people – not just those who go on to work in marketing, but perhaps even more importantly those who become finance officers, management consultants, and CEOs. The second is the way in which advertising theory is mediated through advertising research. There is an enormous world market for research that sets out to measure the effectiveness of advertising, perhaps even more so before the event (pre-testing, or copy-testing), than after it. Copy-testing research inevitably involves operationalising a theory about how advertising, or at least a particular advertisement, is expected to work, whether or not that theory is articulated or consciously chosen or not. Advertising academics, therefore, have an important responsibility for the way both these channels are shaped.

Not all advertising academics, of course, think the same. There is a wide spectrum of different approaches and many findings are hard to reconcile with each other. It is possible however to group different theories together and identify some main streams of thought. Let's look at two attempts at doing this that have been published. One is the section on 'How Advertising Works' in Aaker, Batra and Myers's textbook *Advertising Management*; the other, much more comprehensive but a denser read, is a 1999 review paper by Vakratsas and Ambler, 'How Advertising Works: What do we Really Know?'. One thing that may strike you about both these overviews is that the cast of characters is very different from the present book. Although Vakratsas and Ambler give over 250 references, you won't find Hopkins, Dichter, Gallup, Starch, Bernbach or James Webb Young – and certainly no Watzlawick or Barnum! - while Reeves and Ogilvy are mentioned only in passing. Instead you'll find names like Zajonc, Krugman, Holbrook, and quite often, Petty and Cacioppo, who I can promise you virtually no-one in an ad agency has ever heard of. Also some of the language is different - words like *cognition*, *affect*, and *elaboration* loom large. Underneath it all, however, there are parallels between these taxonomies of academic theories and the different models presented in this book. Vakratsas and Ambler classify theories of advertising as to whether they are based on cognition (conscious mental process), affect (roughly, feelings), experience, or various combinations of these three constructs. *Very* loosely, theories that are led by cognition can be mapped on to my various 'salesmanship' models, and those led by affect to my 'seduction' models - though it's a bit more complicated than that.

And as with the history of practitioner theory, the cognitive/conscious persuasion type models have traditionally won and kept the high ground. Probably for similar reasons; they're easier to understand, they make neater flow charts, they lend themselves to measurement and experiment, and they don't evoke thoughts of mumbo-jumbo or Hidden Persuaders. Meanwhile those who prefer to think that advertising doesn't work by conscious persuasion (or at least, not much), have always been on the periphery, if not downright heretics.

Recently, however, they may have been gaining some real ground. Leading the challenge to the dominant, cognitive processing paradigm has been Dr Robert Heath, a former account planner and now Associate Professor of Advertising Theory at the University of Bath School of Management. Heath's PhD thesis rigorously built the case that what he has called 'Low Attention Processing', far from being at best an inferior means of persuasion, is in many ways more powerful and effective precisely because people are not aware that they are being influenced. His recent book, *Seducing the Subconscious*, builds further on this argument, developing a coherent (if complex) psychological theory with empirical support for a range of propositions that most advertising people have long believed to be true, but didn't have the theory or evidence to support. This is a good example of how academic rigour and hard thought can open up more possibilities for practitioners.

Appendix 2:

Use of 'motivation research' and 'hidden persuaders'.

The chart below shows use of each phrase as recorded in the combined American and British English corpora of Google Books using their Ngram Viewer:

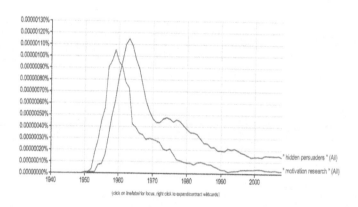

See http://books.google.com/ngrams for more detail.

Bibliography

I have not attempted to encumber this text with a full scholarly apparatus, but I hope it will be clear enough as to which sources I have used. I list below all the main works I have consulted, and all books referred to. I have only cited references thus (Mattelart and Mattelart) when the source is not already mentioned in the text. Where possible I give page references for quotes. Unattributed quotes from Bill Bernbach come from a little book published many years ago by DDB (not dated), Bill Bernbach Said. I have relied heavily on Mayer and Fox throughout, so unless otherwise indicated most of the detail on advertising and research history is from them. I wish I had discovered Roland Marchand's great study of US advertising in the twenties and thirties before I had almost finished my book: I can recommend it, along with Mayer and Fox, as a corrective to my own simplifications. The chapter on PR owes much to Ewen and to Miller's introduction to Bernays's Propaganda, and the section on Barnum is largely based on Cook.

Aaker, D., Batra, R., Myers, J. (1992). *Advertising Management (Fourth Edition)*. Englewood Cliffs, NJ: Prentice-Hall.

Ariely, D. (2008). *Predictably Irrational: the Hidden Forces that Shape our Decisions*. London: Harper Collins.

Barden, P. (2013). *Decoded: The Science Behind Why We Buy*. Chichester: John Wiley & Sons.

Bernays, E. (2005). *Propaganda: with an introduction by Mark Crispin Miller*. Brooklyn, NY: Ig Publishing.

Bernbach, W. (1971). Bill Bernbach defines the four disciplines of creativity. *Advertising Age* 7/5/71.

Bernbach, W. (1980). Facts are not Enough. Paper from the 1980 Meeting of AAAA, May 14-18, White Sulphur Springs, West Virginia.

Binet, L., and Field, P. (2007). *Marketing in the Age of Accountability*. Henley-on-Thames: WARC.

Bonnange, C., and Thomas, C. (1987). *Don Juan ou Pavlov: Essai sur la communication publicitaire*. Paris: Éditions du Seuil. [This fascinating French book is the only place I have seen Watzlawick's axioms applied to advertising before I discovered them. I am most grateful to my former DDB colleague, Marta Insua, for introducing me both to this book and to Watzlawick's work.]

Cady, E., ed. (1966). *The American Poets 1800-1900*. Glenview, Ill.: Scott, Foresman and Co.

Cialdini, R. (1984). *Influence: The Psychology of Persuasion*. New York: Harper Collins.

Colley, R. (1961). *Defining Advertising Goals for Measured Advertising Results*. New York: Association of National Advertisers.

Cook, J.W. (2005, Ed.). *The Colossal P.T. Barnum Reader*. Urbana, Ill: University of Illinois Press.

Cracknell, A. (2011). *The Real Mad Men*. London: Quercus.

Crimmins, J. and Anschuetz, N. (2003). Contagious Demand. Proceedings of MRS Conference, Brighton.

Damasio, A. (1996). *Descartes' Error: Emotion, Reason and the Human Brain*. London: Papermac.

Delaney, S. (2007). *Get Smashed: The story of the men who made the adverts that changed our lives*. London: Sceptre.

Dichter, E. (1979). *Getting Motivated by Ernest Dichter*. New York: Pergamon Press.

Dragon, R. (2011). The AIDA Model and St Elmo Lewis. http://www.dragonsearchmarketing.com/who-created-aida/

Earls, M. (2007). *Herd: How to Change Mass Behaviour by Harnessing our True Nature*. Chichester: John Wiley & Sons.

Ewen, S. (1996). *PR! A Social History of Spin*. New York: Basic Books.

Feldwick, P. (2007). Account Planning: its history and Significance for Ad Agencies. Chapter 3.3 in Tellis, G. and Ambler, T., *The SAGE Handbook of Advertising*. Los Angeles: Sage Publications, pp.184-198.

Feldwick, P. (2009). Brand Communications. Chapter 9 in Clifton, R. (ed), *Brands and Branding (Second Edition)*. London: The Economist/Profile Books, pp.127-145.

Fletcher, W. (2008). *Powers of Persuasion: The Inside Story of British Advertising 1951-2000*. Oxford: University Press.

Fox, S. (1990). *The Mirror Makers: A History of American Advertising*. London: Heinemann.

Gardner, B. and Levy, S. (1955). The Product and the Brand. *Harvard Business Review*, March-April, pp.33-39.

Grant, J. (2002). *After Image: Mind-Altering Marketing*. London: Harper Collins.

Gunther, J. (1960). *Taken at the Flood: The Story of Albert D. Lasker*. London: Hamish Hamilton.

Heath, R. (2001). *The Hidden Power of Advertising*. Henley-on-Thames: Admap Publications.

Heath, R. (2012). *Seducing the Subconscious: The Psychology of Emotional Influence in Advertising*. Chichester: Wiley-Blackwell.

Heath, R. and Feldwick, P. (2008). Fifty Years Using the Wrong Model of Advertising. *International Journal of Market Research*, 50:1, pp. 29-59.

Henry, H. (1958). *Motivation Research*. London: Crosby, Lockwood & Son.

Hillman, J. (1995). *Kinds of Power: A Guide to its Intelligent Uses*. New York: Currency Doubleday.

Hopkins, C. (1923 and 1927/1986). *Scientific Advertising* and *My Life in Advertising*. Chicago: NTC Business Books.

Joyce, T. (1967). What do we know about how advertising works? In Broadbent, S. ed. (1980), *Market Researchers Look at Advertising*. London: Sigmatext. pp. 27-38.

Kahneman, D. (2011). *Thinking, fast and slow*. London: Allen Lane.

Krech, D., Crutchfield, R., and Ballachey, E. (1962). *Individual in Society: A Textbook of Social Psychology*. Tokyo: McGraw-Hill Kogakusha, Ltd.

Keynes, J. (1936). *The General Theory of Employment, Interest and Money*. London: Macmillan & Co. [The quotation given comes from the concluding paragraph of the book.]

Lannon, J. and Baskin, M. (2007). *A Master Class in Brand Planning: The Timeless Works of Stephen King*. Chichester: John Wiley & Sons.

Martineau, P. (1957). *Motivation in Advertising: Motives that Make People Buy*. New York: McGraw-Hill.

Marchand, R. (1985). *Advertising the American Dream: Making Way for Modernity, 1920-1940.* Berkeley, Ca: University of California Press.

Mattelart, A. and Mattelart, M. (1998). *Theories of Communication: A Short Introduction.* London: Sage.

Mayer, M. (1958) *Madison Avenue, USA: the Inside Story of American Advertising.* London: The Bodley Head.

McQueen, A. (2011).*The King of Sunlight: How William Lever cleaned up the world.* London: Corgi.

Morgan, G. (2006). *Images of Organization (Updated Edition).* Thousand Oaks, CA: Sage.

Ogilvy, D. (1983). *Ogilvy on Advertising.* London: Pan Books.

Packard, V. (1957). *The Hidden Persuaders: An introduction to the techniques of mass-persuasion through the unconscious.* London: Longmans, Green & Co.

Reeves, R. (1961/1986). *Reality in Advertising (sixteenth printing).* New York: Alfred A. Knopf.

Ridderstråle, J. and Nordström, K. (2000). *Funky Business: Talent Makes Capital Dance.* London: FT Prentice Hall.

Robinson, J. (1998). *The Manipulators: Unmasking the Hidden Persuaders.* London: Pocket Books.

Schwartz, B. (2004). *The Paradox of Choice: Why More is Less.* New York: Harper Perennial.

Scase, R. (2010). The iPod generation looks for honesty, not marketing spin. *Market Leader,* Q1, p.21.

Scott, W. (1903/1921). *The Psychology of Advertising in Theory and Practice.* Boston: Small, Maynard & Co.

Sharp, B. (2010). *How Brands Grow: What Marketers Don't Know.* South Melbourne: Oxford University Press.

Starch, D. (1923). *Principles of Advertising.* Chicago: A.W.Shaw.

Sumner, G. (1953). *How I Learned the Secrets of Success in Advertising*. Kingswood, Surrey: The World's Work Ltd.

Thaler, R., and Sunstein, C. (2008). *Nudge: Improving Decisions About Health, Wealth, and Happiness*. New Haven: Yale University Press.

Toulmin, S. (1990). *Cosmopolis: The Hidden Agenda of Modernity*. Chicago: University of Chicago Press.

Tuck, M. (1971). Practical Frameworks for Advertising and Research. In Broadbent, S. ed. (1980). *Market Researchers Look at Advertising*. London: Sigmatext. pp. 51-62.

Vakratsas, D. and Ambler, T. (1999). How Advertising Works: What Do We Really Know? *Journal of Marketing*, 63:1 (January), pp.26-43.

Watzlawick, P., Bavelas, J. and Jackson, D. (1967). *Pragmatics of Human Communication*. New York: W.W.Norton & Co.

Wilson, T. (2002). *Strangers to Ourselves: Discovering the Adaptive Unconscious*. Cambridge, Mass: The Belknap Press of Harvard University Press.

Wolpert, L. (1992). *The Unnatural Nature of Science*. London: Faber and Faber.

Young, J. (1963/1979). *How to Become an Advertising Man*. Chicago: Crain Books (reprint).

INDEX

9 781784 621926